THE COMPLETE BOOK OF
SEWING

THE COMPLETE BOOK OF
SEWING

FULL STEP-BY-STEP TECHNIQUES AND 15 SIMPLE PATTERNS

WENDY GARDINER

NH
NEW
HOLLAND

Published in 2007 by
New Holland Publishers (UK) Ltd
London · Cape Town · Sydney · Auckland
www.newhollandpublishers.com

Garfield House
86–88 Edgware Road
London W2 2EA
United Kingdom

80 McKenzie Street
Cape Town 8001
South Africa

Level 1, Unit 4, 14 Aquatic Drive
Frenchs Forest, NSW 2086
Australia

218 Lake Road
Northcote, Auckland
New Zealand

ISBN 978 1 84537 286 6

Senior Editor: Clare Sayer
Production: Hazel Kirkman
Design: Peter Crump
Photographer: Sian Irvine
Illustrations: Coral Mula
Pattern diagrams: Stephen Dew
Editorial Direction: Rosemary Wilkinson

10 9 8 7 6 5 4 3 2 1

Reproduction by Pica Digital PTE Ltd, Singapore
Printed and bound by Times Offset (M) Sdn Bhd,
Malaysia

ACKNOWLEDGEMENTS

Special thanks to Past Time Fabrics for the fabrics used in
all the samples throughout the book and to John Kaldor
Fabrics for the fabric for the Dressing up tunics, Timeless
trousers, Casual shorts, Evening skirt, Long cardigan coat,
Simple summer dress and Negligée. Thanks also to
Simplicity and Burda Patterns for patterns and drafting
paper, Janome for the loan of their sewing machines and
Gutermann and Groves & Banks for thread and
haberdashery respectively. For a full list of suppliers and
addresses, see page 158.

Also, many thanks to my contributors who designed and
made the following projects: Lynne Garner for the Simple
shell top, Edge-to-edge jacket, Fleece gilet, Timeless
trousers and Casual shorts; Joan Irvine for the Classic
bustier, Bustier with straps and Long cardigan coat; Alison
Smith for the three skirt projects and Lorna Knight for the
Simple summer dress and Negligée.

Contents

SEWING ESSENTIALS

BASIC TECHNIQUES

STYLE TECHNIQUES

PROJECTS

Sewing essentials

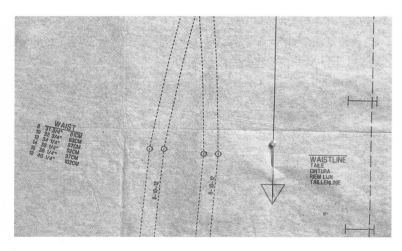

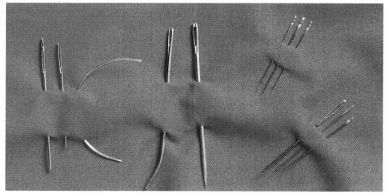

Sewing machines

There is a huge range of sewing machines available today, ranging from basic models that do straight and zigzag stitch, to computerized embroidery machines that can stitch beautiful embroidery designs that you have customized yourself.

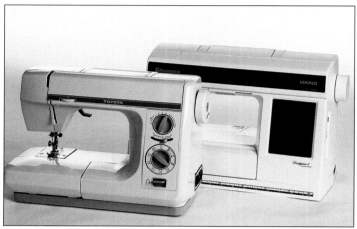

BASIC AND COMPUTERIZED SEWING MACHINES

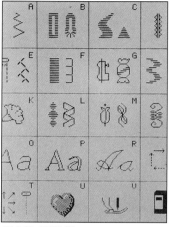

AN LCD DISPLAY

A sewing machine helps you to stitch faster, creating neat even stitching time after time. Using the correct feet (see page 11) also helps with different types of sewing, whether it is inserting a zipper or creating perfectly formed buttonholes every time. Using different stitches that are built-in to the sewing machine enables you to embellish and customize by adding decorative stitching, trims and fringing.

How they work

Electronic models stitch automatically when pressure is applied to the foot pedal – the heavier the pressure, the faster the machine stitches. Stitch choice, length and width are chosen by changing the direction of dials or buttons, usually located on the front of

the machine. They might also have a small LCD screen to show selections made.

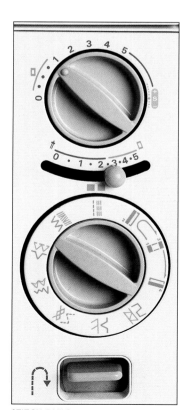

STITCH DIALS

Computerized models are fully automated – they automatically set the correct stitch tension, length and width for the stitch you have chosen on the LCD touch screen. The screen also displays the recommended foot, and the option to change the stitch length or width etc. to suit your own preferences. For instance, you may select a straight stitch, but want to increase the stitch length to maximum in order to make a gathering stitch. The automatic tension means that you can sew a single layer of flimsy fabric as evenly as multi-layers of denim or fleece. Computerized models also have a variety of embroidery designs and alphabets built in.

Choosing a new sewing machine

Which type of sewing machine you buy will depend on budget, type of sewing and personal preference. However, always buy the best you can afford, even if it has more features than you need at the moment – you can grow in to them. The following are a few basic guidelines to consider when choosing a new machine:

• Try out different models in your budget range to see how they sew different weights and types of fabric. Take your own fabric samples to try.

• Check the ease of threading both top thread and bobbin. Can the bobbin be wound with thread without unthreading the top thread and needle? Useful if a new bobbin is needed in the middle of a seam! Drop-in bobbins are less awkward than rotary hook bobbins.

• Most modern machines have snap-on feet, which makes changing feet for different sewing techniques much easier. Check what feet are included in the basic price and what optional extras are available. Essentials are straight stitch, buttonhole, zipper, blind-hem, darning/free motion, appliqué.

- Look for a variable stitch speed which allows you to control how fast or slow you stitch. This is very important when stitching around tricky curves and corners or applying appliqué.
- If you intend to sew soft furnishings and other large projects, check the size of the aperture between the body of the machine and the needle. Bigger is better in order to fit large quantities of fabric through. Equally, a wide flatbed surface helps guide fabric. Some machines have an optional extension table.
- If you intend to carry your machine to workshops, check the weight and portability. What type of cover does it have? Note that computerized machines are much heavier than electronic machines.
- Ask about warranty, servicing and repair facilities. Many manufacturers offer a 3–5 year warranty.
- Ask about courses, workshops and after-sales service. Many manufacturers offer tutorials as part of the purchase price.
- How easy will it be to update a computerized model? Technology continues to advance, bringing new developments and stitch choices – can your preferred model be updated?

Threading

Each sewing machine looks slightly different depending on the model and manufacturer. However, the main principles are the same on all. Check your user's manual to determine where the relevant features are on your model.

Upper thread

Most machines have one or two upper thread spindles on which the thread reel is placed; these may be vertical or horizontal. Which way round to place the reel (with thread coming over the top or from under the reel) is important because it can affect the way the machine stitches, so check your user's manual. Once the thread is on the spindle, add a thread retainer to keep the reel from bouncing up and down the spindle when it revolves (which will cause uneven stitching or broken threads). The thread is then taken from the reel, through a guide loop on the top of the machine, down, then up through tension discs before being fed behind a hook on the needle column and then threaded from the front to the back of the needle (diagram 1).

Bobbins

Whilst you can buy universal bobbins, it is preferable to use those that are supplied with the machine because some models get temperamental if using other types of bobbin. Bobbins can be wound with the same thread as the upper thread or with a special bobbin fill if doing machine embroidery or lots of appliqué (bobbin fill is finer, making it

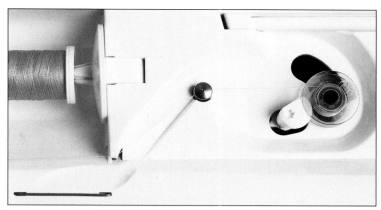

WINDING A BOBBIN

ideal for heavily concentrated stitch areas). Place the bobbin on the bobbin winder spindle (at the front or the side of the machine) and push the spindle into the wind position. On modern machines this disengages the needle and allows you to wind bobbins without unthreading the upper thread (check your user's manual). Use the bobbin winder for general sewing thread to ensure an evenly wound bobbin. If it is too loosely wound or uneven, it may cause the bobbin to jam when sewing, which can cause broken or uneven stitching. (Note if using speciality threads for a decorative finish, hand-wind them onto the bobbin and then stitch slowly.) Clean the bobbin area frequently using the brush provided in the tool kit to prevent fluff build up (which can jam the machine).

DIAGRAM 1

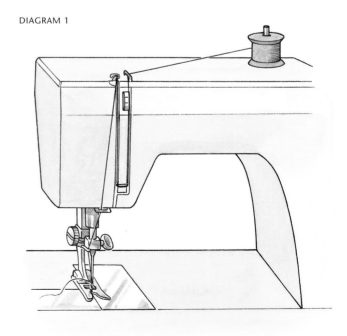

Starting to stitch

It is preferable to bring up the bobbin thread before you start to stitch to prevent the threads tangling at the start of a seam. To raise the bobbin thread, turn the fly wheel by hand to lower and raise the needle. As the upper thread comes back up, pull it from behind the needle to bring up the bobbin thread loop and then pull both together to create a 5–8 cm (2–3 in) thread tail.

Helpful hint: *To ensure the fabric is not pulled down into the throat plate and to prevent threads tangling at the start of stitching, hold the thread tails at the back when making the first few stitches.*

Helpful hint: *Stitch tension is correct when the upper thread shows on the top of the fabric and the bobbin thread shows on the underside. The two threads are interlocked between the fabric layers (diagram 2).*

HOLD THE THREAD TAILS WHEN STARTING TO STITCH

DIAGRAM 2

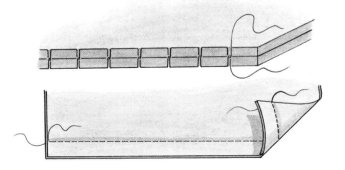

Stitch length

An average stitch length for medium-weight fabric is 2.5–3 mm or 10–12 spi (stitches per inch). Stitch length is altered by a dial on electronic machines, or by tapping the increase/decrease points on the LCD screen of a computerized model. There will be a minimum and maximum stitch length – minimum is used to stitch on the spot and maximum for basting or gathering stitches. Shorter stitch lengths are used for finer fabrics and longer stitch lengths are used for sewing bulkier fabrics.

STITCH LENGTH GUIDE	
Fabric	**Stitch length**
Very lightweight fabrics – voiles/organza/chiffon	2–2.5 mm or 10–12 spi
General sewing cottons, polycottons etc.	2.5–3 mm or 8–10 spi
Medium weight wools, worsteds, gabardine	3–3.5 mm or 7–8 spi
Heavyweight wools, tweeds, fleece	3.5–5 mm or 5–7 spi

Stitch width

The stitch width is only applicable on stitches that have a sideways element, such as zigzag stitch or decorative stitches. Adjust with the dial or LCD screen as for length, reducing or increasing to suit the fabric weight and stitch choice.

Helpful hint: *Test stitch the length and width on a sample made up of the same number of layers and interfacings etc. Adjust the length/width as necessary to achieve an even, straight row of stitching.*

Guide to other machine parts

Flywheel – Also known as the balance wheel. Turn it to lower and raise the needle, step by step.

Needle – Sewing machine needles have a flat surface on one side of the shaft. For most machines, this is placed in the thread column facing to the back. To secure the needle in position, tighten the screw with the screwdriver provided in the tool kit.

Presser foot – This is used to help keep the fabric in position as it is fed through when being stitched. Snap-on feet are easy to remove and replace. The presser foot is lifted or lowered using a lever on the side or back of the foot column or by computerized button.

Feed dogs – Positioned under the presser foot, these raised jagged edges move back and forth when the machine is in use in order to feed the fabric as it is being stitched. Lowering the feed dogs disengages them and thus

enables you to move the fabric in any direction as it is being stitched.

Throat plate (or needle plate) – This metal plate has a central hole which fits over the feed dogs and provides a space for the needle to go down and pick up the bobbin thread. The different markings are used as a guide for seam width. Alternative throat plates with smaller apertures are available for some models.

Flat bed and free arm – These are the terms for the sewing surface. The flat bed usually incorporates the tool kit/machine accessory case which can be removed to make the sewing surface. The free arm is a thinner base used when sewing small items, such as cuffs or trouser hems.

Presser feet

Every sewing machine is provided with a basic range of feet which help sew specific techniques, such as a general purpose foot, zipper foot and buttonhole foot. Other feet are usually available as optional extras. Each has

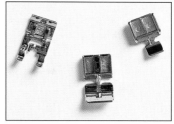
GENERAL PURPOSE AND ZIPPER FEET

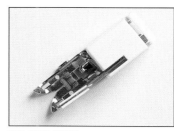
WALKING FOOT

EMBROIDERY FOOT, BLIND HEM FOOT AND OVERCASTING FOOT

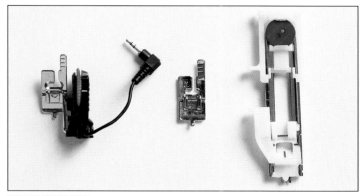
BUTTONHOLE FEET

different widths, grooves underneath to move smoothly over concentrated stitch areas, or hooks and angles through which trims, piping etc. can be fed.

General purpose foot – The most frequently used foot, ideal for straight stitching.

Zipper foot – These can vary in appearance, but all are designed to allow stitching close to the zipper teeth.

Buttonhole foot – These vary from model to model. Some have a slot to insert a button at the back. The underside has deep grooves to allow it to glide over dense stitching.

Embroidery/appliqué/satin stitch foot – Usually clear plastic, a wide groove on the underside helps the foot glide over concentrated stitching.

Blind hem foot – Used to machine stitch blind hems, the foot has a metal guide against which the folded fabric is fed.

Overcasting foot – Designed to stitch at the edge of the fabric, it has a wire brush on the underside to prevent the fabric edge from rolling or puckering.

Walking foot – Although large and cumbersome to look at, this foot helps feed fabric layers through evenly and is ideal for fabrics with a pile such as fur, or for accurately matching plaids and quilting several layers.

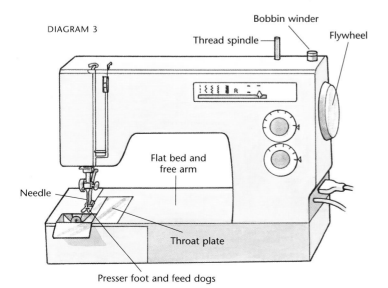
DIAGRAM 3

Bobbin winder
Thread spindle
Flywheel
Flat bed and free arm
Needle
Throat plate
Presser foot and feed dogs

Sergers

Sergers (also known as overlockers) are ideal for fast sewing because they stitch, trim fabric from the seam allowance and neaten all at the same time. They use between 2–8 threads to complete the process, depending on the stitch technique and type of serger. The most common machines have three or four threads whilst the top of the range have eight thread positions and the option to cover stitch as well as serge. Serged seams are flexible, making them ideal for stretchy fabrics, sportswear and lingerie.

How sergers work

Sergers do not have bobbins, but have one or two needles and two loopers instead. The needles stitch straight rows of stitching, whilst the upper and lower loopers form the overcast stitch along the cut edge, interlocking at the very edge. All four are threaded through individual thread tensions with cones or cops of thread held on spindles at the back of the machine. It is often necessary to thread in a specific sequence in order to make the machine stitch properly (check your user's manual for threading guide).

Sergers also have cutting blades positioned to the right of the needle, so that when the machine is operated, the fabric edge is cut before it continues to feed under the foot to be stitched and overlocked. The blades can be lowered to disengage them if desired.

Modern sergers also have differential feed, which means that they evenly feed fabric layers at the same time, avoiding overstretched or puckered seams.

Sergers can be used simply to neaten seams quickly and efficiently, or to create decorative finishes when using the special feet available, such as creating a rolled hem, gathering, attaching bindings and piping. Although feet and needles carry out the same function as on sewing machines, they are rarely interchangeable.

Serger thread is usually finer and comes on large cones or cops (sometimes called bobbins, but not to be confused with sewing machine bobbins) because serging uses far more thread than a sewing machine. If using speciality threads, use them in the loopers which have larger-eyed needles.

FABRIC THAT HAS BEEN OVERLOCKED

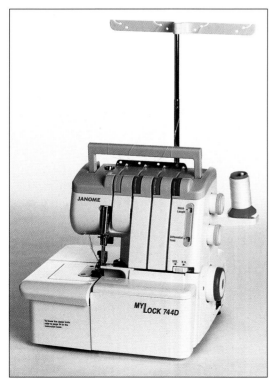

A SERGER

A BLADE CUTS THE FABRIC BEFORE STITCHING

SERGER CONES

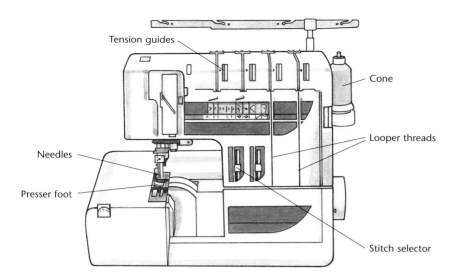

Tension guides

Cone

Needles

Looper threads

Presser foot

Stitch selector

The different parts of the serger

Needles – A three-thread serger has one needle whereas a four-thread machine has two needles and a five-thread may have three needles. A three-thread machine stitches a straight line and overlocks the edge in one pass which is generally only used for seam neatening. The four-thread serger with two needles stitches a seam plus a parallel straight line and overlocked edge making it a stronger combination, useful for complete garment or project construction. Needles can be removed if the stitch technique doesn't require all needles in operation, as in flat

Helpful hint: Before changing or removing needles, place fabric under the presser foot so that the needle cannot accidentally drop down through the throat plate.

locking which requires one needle only.

Loopers – The function of the loopers is to form the overlocked stitching at the fabric edge. The looper threads go through their own thread guides, which take them under the needle plate. Threading the loopers can be tricky. The lower looper thread forms the stitching on the underside of the work and the upper looper thread forms the stitching on the top.

Thread guide – Each is usually colour coded so that the correct needle or looper thread trail is easier to follow. Cones are placed on spindles at the back of the machine and should then be covered with nets (provided in the tool kit) to prevent threads unravelling from the cones unevenly. The thread guide at the back can be raised when in use and lowered for storage.

Thread tensions – Some models have automatic thread tensions on all threads, others have dials to alter the tensions individually. Those with dials

usually have shaded or marked optimum tension settings. Tensions may need to be altered when using different stitch techniques or stitching very fine or very bulky fabric. If the looper stitches do not interlock on the fabric edge, the upper looper tension may be too tight, or lower looper too loose. Tighten and loosen the tensions a little at a time.

Stitch selector – As with sewing machines, sergers have stitch options in order to create different finishes. Your

user's manual will advise on any tension alterations and the recommended foot and needles.

Starting to stitch

Always test the stitching on a sample before working on the main project. Start stitching before the fabric is fed through in order to create a chain of stitches 8–10 cm (3–5 in) long. Then, holding the chain at the back of the machine, feed the fabric under the foot (which can be left down or raised to start). Always have the blade at its highest point when starting (turn the balance wheel by hand to raise it). At the seam end, continue stitching for a further 8–10 cm (3–5 in) to create another chain of stitches. Use a bodkin (large eyed needle) to thread this chain back through the overlocked edge.

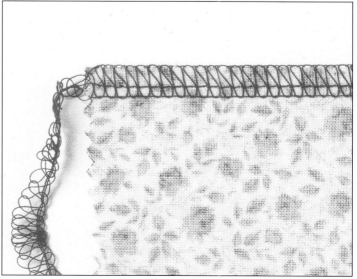

LEAVE A THREAD TAIL AT THE END

Fabrics

There is a huge range of fabrics available for dressmaking, crafts and soft furnishings. Which to use and when depends on the type of project, whether you want something bold and dramatic or classic and understated. Most important is to use the right type and weight of fabric. Below is a list of the common fabric types and their uses.

Lightweight fabrics

Many different fabrics are available in lightweight varieties, including cottons, voiles, linens, silks, woollens and polycotton mixes. Most are stable, woven fabrics that are easy to sew. Cotton, linen, silk and wool are made from natural fibres, which are often mixed with man-made fibres to create fabrics that are stronger and more crease-resistant.

Use general-purpose thread and neaten seams with overcast stitch, zigzag stitch or pinking shears. Pure cottons and linens can be pressed with a hot iron. For silks, wools and mixed fibre fabrics, always use a press cloth and medium to hot iron. Use a 70–80 (10–12) universal needle.

Common fabric types

Batiste – Lightweight, soft and sheer, batiste can be made in cotton, wool or synthetic fibres. Used for underlinings, quilt backing and heirloom sewing.

Calico – A plain woven, inexpensive cream-coloured cotton fabric. Different weights are available. Used for quilting or making toiles (test garments).

Chambray – Similar in appearance to denim,

SELECTION OF LIGHTWEIGHT FABRICS

BRODERIE ANGLAISE

Chambray is normally cotton, although sometimes mixed with other fibres. Used for shirts and childrenswear.

Cheesecloth – A cotton fabric, loosely woven with a slightly crinkled surface. Used for crafts, casual gypsy-style tops and other fashion items.

Chiffon – A light, drapable sheer fabric that can be pure silk or synthetic. Used for blouses, over-skirts and wraps.

Cottons, polyester/cotton – Very versatile, easy to sew and available in a huge colour range, both in plains and prints. Used for summer clothing, craft projects and quilting.

Cotton lawn – Lightweight and crisp to handle. Used for christening gowns, heirloom stitching and linings.

Eyelet embroidery (broderie anglaise) – Traditionally a cotton fabric, it has a light self-coloured pattern which incorporates stitched eyelets. Used for childrenswear, summer tops, full skirts and nightwear.

Gingham – A check fabric, usually cotton. Used for dresses, blouses, craft projects and café-style curtains.

Georgette – A sheer fabric, similar to chiffon but made with crêpe yarns for a more dense finish. Used for blouses and wraps.

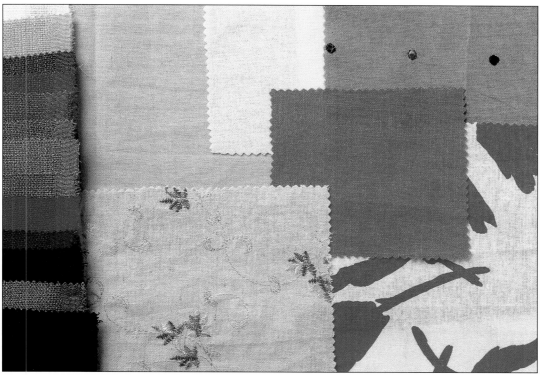

LINEN AND LINEN MIX FABRICS

Linen – Easily creased, linens can be very lightweight (handkerchief linen) or medium-weight when mixed with other fibres (linen-like) which makes them more crease-resistant and stable. Handkerchief linen is used for tops and table linen. Linen and linen-like is used for smart suits, dresses, trousers and jackets.

Muslin – A lightweight, plain weave fabric. Used for crafts, lightweight curtains and interfacings.

Organza/organdie – Slightly crisper than chiffon, organza is also sheer and often made of polyester or silk. Used for wraps and crisp blouses.

Polyester, polyester crêpe de chine, viscose, rayon – Man-made, these fabrics can range from light- to medium-weight. They look and feel like natural fibre fabrics, but with greater strength, crease-resistance and wearability. However, polyesters do fray easily so seam neatening is crucial. Used in the same way as silks, cottons and wools, depending on weight.

Poplin – Slightly heavier and crisper than cotton lawn, poplin is woven with a fine horizontal rib. Used for summerwear and childrenswear.

Seersucker – Lightweight, usually cotton, seersucker has alternating stripes that are puckered and crinkled. Used for lightweight jackets and tops.

Silks – There are many silk varieties, including crêpe de chine, raw silk, shantung, thai silk, silk noil, china silk, polyester, viscose and rayon silks. Raw silks, shantung and noils have some surface texture and shading. Treat as a pile fabric and use 'with nap' layouts. Silks can range from light- to medium-weight. Used for dressmaking and luxury soft furnishings. China silk is used for linings.

Taffeta/moiré taffeta – Originally made from silk, taffetas can also be polyester. They have a crisp finish and shiny surface. Moiré taffeta has a 'water mark' pattern. Used for eveningwear, wraps and bridalwear.

Tulle – Made from silk, nylon or other man-made fibres, tulle is a fine net. Used for bridal veils and fancy-dress costumes.

Voile – A sheer, lightweight plain weave fabric, some have iridescent fibres for added shimmer. Used for lightweight drapes and summer wraps.

Medium-weight fabrics

These include fabrics suitable for dressmaking, craft and soft furnishings such as wools, wool mixes, heavier silks, satins and cottons with textured weave. Most are easy to sew, stable woven fabrics.

Use general-purpose thread and neaten seams with overcast stitch, zigzag stitch or bound seams. Alternatively, sew with special seams such as flat fell or French (see Seams, page 50). Always use a press cloth and steam. Allow to cool before handling. Use size 80 (12) needles.

Common fabric types

Angora, alpaca – Luxury soft wool fabrics: angora comes from goat hair and alpaca from llama. Angora is often mixed with other fibres to create a woollen cloth. Used for knitwear and woollen coating.

Challis – Woven with a crêpe yarn to give an all-over crinkled surface. Wool challis is a luxury fabric, it breathes well and creases very little. Often printed with paisley or floral designs. Used for dresses, jackets, A-line or full skirts.

Chintz – A cotton fabric that is closely woven and has a glazed finished. Used for crafts, table linen and soft furnishings.

Corduroy – Has a sheared rib surface and can be pure cotton or a mix of fibres. Rib size can vary from narrow baby cord to thick elephant cord. Use 'with nap' layouts. Used for trousers, jackets, vests etc.

SELECTION OF MEDIUM-WEIGHT FABRICS

CRÊPE BACK SATIN

Flannel – Can be plain or twill weave, both having a soft brushed surface on one or both sides. Used for jackets, suits, skirts and trousers.

Gabardine – A close twill weave gives the distinctive surface pattern. Made from a variety of fibres and wool blends, it is water-repellent and hardwearing. Used for suits, trousers, skirts, jackets and coats.

Satin/duchesse satin – A high sheen, smooth fabric. Use 'with nap' layout to prevent unwanted shading. Duchesse satin has a very high lustre. Used for bridal and evening wear.

Wool crêpe – Has a twisted weave which creates surface texture. Different weights and varieties are available, better qualities are more crease-resistant. Crêpe can shrink when laundered, so pre-shrink before cutting out. Used for suits, tailored skirts and trousers, jackets and dresses.

Drill – A strong twill weave and heavier weight cotton. Canvas is a similar fabric. Used for outdoor and hardwearing items.

Dupion – Has a thick uneven texture created by two fibres of silk woven together. Can also be made from synthetic fibres. Used for lightweight jackets, dresses and tops.

Crêpe back satin – Also known as satin back crêpe, this is a double-sided fabric with twisted crêpe weave on one side and a smooth shiny satin on the other. Used for evening wear, bridal wear, smart trousers, jackets and dresses.

Damask – Traditionally made from linen or cotton on a jacquard loom to produce a self pattern. Used for table linen and home furnishings.

Denim – A twill weave fabric that is now available in many different colours and weights. The very distinctive twill weave is created by a coloured warp and white weft. Used for trousers, jackets and skirts, depending on the weight.

DENIM FABRICS

Heavyweight fabrics

Many fabric types have heavyweight varieties, such as woollens, tweeds, bouclés and fleece. Many also have a one-way sheen or pile, such as cashmere, so always use the 'with nap' layout. Use a press cloth and minimal steam and press from the wrong side whenever possible. For very fluffy, hairy fabrics, use a towel as a pressing surface to prevent the pile flattening when pressed. Trim the pile from the seam allowances to reduce bulk. Use lining fabrics for facings to avoid unnecessary bulk at collars, cuffs etc. Use size 70–80 (10–12) universal needles and medium- to heavyweight interfacings. Use sew-in interfacings on pile fabrics.

Common fabric types

Boiled wool – A felted knitted fabric. Create your own by machine washing and drying a loosely woven knit wool. Fabric will shrink by 40–50% in both directions. Used for jackets, fitted tops and coats.
Bouclé – Can be knitted or woven, usually with a dull textural thick nobbly surface. Used for jackets, vests and coats.
Brocade – Incorporates a jacquard design of flowers, leaves or geometric patterns to create a raised surface contrast or colour. Used for bridal- or eveningwear and table linen.

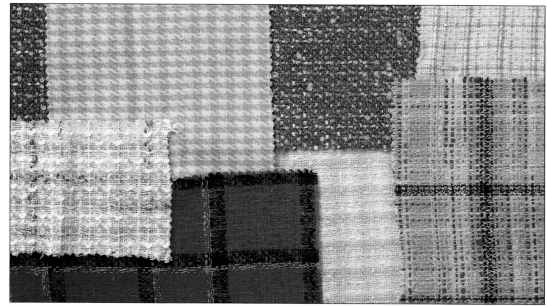

SELECTION OF HEAVYWEIGHT FABRICS

BOUCLE FABRIC

Camel hair – Woven from the under hair of a camel, it is often mixed with sheep's wool, for greater durability. It is a luxury fabric with a distinctive soft yellow colour. Used for coats and jackets.

Cashmere – Made from the hair of Kashmir goats, this very fine, soft fabric is comfortable to wear. Cashmere can be knitted or woven. Used for coats, scarves and sweaters.

Chenille – Soft to touch, with a raised surface texture. Good drapability but inclined to stretch. Fully interface with a fusible interfacing. Used for vests, jackets, loose tunic tops and bathrobes.

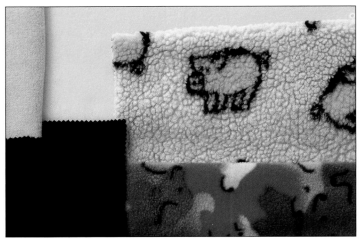

FLEECE FABRICS

KNIT FABRICS

Fleece – Very versatile and easy to sew, available in many colours and designs. Usually polyester, easy care and wear. Use a slightly larger than usual seam allowance to help feed the fabric evenly. No neatening needed. Used for jackets, vests and coats.

Herringbone – Has a twill weave with a distinctive pattern like the backbone of a herring. Used for jackets, coats and suits.

Mohair – Noted for its hairy texture, mohair is a plain weave fabric produced from the fibres of the angora goat. Frequently mixed with wool. Used for coats and jackets.

Tartan – A check, twill weave fabric with a specific check pattern. Careful layout needed to match fabric pattern. Used for kilts, skirts and trousers.

Tweed – Scottish, Irish, Harris and Donegal – Traditional tweeds are thick woollen fabrics with a distinct woven pattern, named after the area of origin. Modern tweed is produced in a wider range of colours and designs. Used for coats, jackets and smart suits.

Worsted – Made from tightly woven woollen yarns, it is hardwearing and usually high quality. Used for suits, coats and upholstery.

Knit fabrics

Knits can be light- to heavyweight depending on the fabric type. They have definite stretch and can be used for close-fitting garments, sportswear and casual wear. Use ball point needles and woven interfacings that can stretch. Stay stitch curved seams. Use edge tape at the neck and armholes to prevent unwanted stretch through prolonged wear. Use zigzag or stretch stitches that allow the fabric to stretch, even when sewn.

Common fabric types

Cotton jersey – A fine lightweight knit fabric which drapes well and is crease-resistant. Orginally only cotton, many other soft knitted fabrics are called jersey. Used for T-shirts, casual dresses and sportswear.

Double knit – A very stable fabric, with vertical ribs on both sides. Available in a wide colour range. Used for sportswear and casual suits.

Lycra and Spandex – Lycra is the trade name for Spandex. This man-made elastic fibre is often combined with other fibres to add stretch. Mixed with cotton it is matt, mixed with nylon it is shiny. Good for very close-fitting, active wear. Used for exercise wear, swimwear and lingerie.

Lamé – Contains a mixture of metallic yarns and can be found in tricot-backed lamé and tissue lamé. It is a fragile fabric which tears easily. Avoid pressing. Used for loose tops, eveningwear, trims and appliqués.

Stretch velour – Sometimes mixed with Lycra, velour is similar to velvet but with a tightly-woven short cut pile. Used for sportswear, robes and kaftans.

TARTAN FABRICS

SPECIALITY FABRICS

Speciality fabrics

These range from synthetic leathers and furs to natural fibre luxury fabrics. Many have piles and textured surfaces so always use 'with nap' layout. Avoid pressing with steam, which can flatten the pile and use a soft towel or velvet board as a pressing surface.

Common fabric types

Faux fur, fun fur – All have pile, some very long, others very short. Use 'with nap' layouts and reduce bulk in the seam allowances by trimming the pile. Use a long stitch length and wider seam allowance to help evenly feed the fabric as it is sewn. Used for coats, jackets and soft furnishings.

Synthetic suede/leather – Similar in look and feel to their natural counterparts, they rarely need neatening. Avoid pins, which will leave holes. Varieties include faux suede, suedette, ultra suede, leatherette and pleather. Use a teflon or coated presser foot to help glide over the fabric. Used for jackets, coats, skirts, trousers and soft furnishings

Velvet – A luxury fabric with a pile that can be made from cotton, silk or man-made fibres. It can be light- or heavyweight. Varieties include panne, chiffon, velveteen, sculptured and devoré. Devoré has a pattern created by parts of the pile being cut or burnt away to reveal the backing. Velvet layers can 'walk'; when sewing, use a walking foot or double pin and baste. Make sure the nap/pile is running in the same direction on all pieces. Used for eveningwear, jackets, trousers and wraps.

Handling fabrics

Having chosen the fabric, the next step is to cut it out, ready to sew. However, there are guidelines you should follow to ensure success. These include understanding and using the fabric grain and using special techniques to sew specialist fabrics.

Grainlines

All woven fabrics have a grain (diagram 1). The grain determines the amount of stretch in the fabric. The lengthwise or straight grain runs parallel with the selvages (side edges). It has the least stretch and therefore most garment pieces are placed with the lengthwise grain running vertically down the pattern piece. The crosswise grain is at right angles to the lengthwise grain and runs from selvage to selvage. It has slightly more give than the lengthwise grain, thus most pattern pieces are laid on the fabric with the cross wise grain going around the body. The bias is any diagonal direction. The true bias runs at a 45-degree angle to the lengthwise grain. Fabric is at its most stretchy along the bias.

Sewing tips for specialist fabrics
General

- Use sharp shears to cut out. Use serrated shears when cutting silks or very fine fabrics. The serrated blades will grip the fabric as it is cut.
- Cut facings from lining fabric rather than heavy pile fabrics or those with beads and sequins.
- Change needles and pins frequently, particularly when sewing fabrics with metallic fibres which can blunt them easily.
- When working with flimsy fabrics, use lots of pins in the seam allowance to keep the layers together.

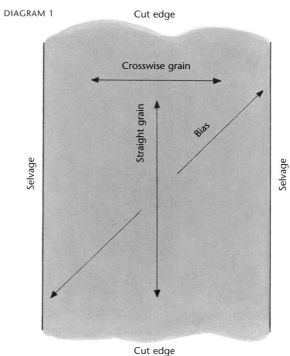

DIAGRAM 1

- When working with faux leather and suede, use weights or tin cans rather than pins which will leave holes.
- Stitch all seams in the direction of the nap whenever possible.
- Use sew-in interfacings.
- Follow the 'with nap' layout to ensure any shading, pile or pattern runs in the same direction.
- Always use a press cloth and press with care. Avoid pressing fabrics that have pre-pressed surface detail such as crushed velvets or pre-pleated fabric.

Checked and striped fabric

- Only use striped or checked fabrics with patterns that list them in the suggested fabrics.
- Make sure the fabric design matches across the garment by placing the paper pattern on a single layer of fabric. Turn the pattern piece over to cut the corresponding section, to get a left and a right piece.
- Make sure the balance marks and notches are in line across all the matching pattern pieces.
- When placing a pattern on fabric, ensure the most dominant stripe or check is not placed at the widest body point, such as the bust or hips. Match checks and stripes at the same point on the pattern pieces. Discount seam allowances when matching patterns.
- It is not possible for checks and stripes to match at all seams, so choose the most prominent places for pattern matching.

Beaded, sequinned fabrics

- Use a zipper foot to stitch beaded fabrics if the beading prevents straight stitching. Use a walking foot to sew heavy pile fabric to help the layers feed evenly.
- To eliminate bulk in the seams, remove beading from the seam allowance by crushing the beads (use a little hammer or two spoons) and gently removing. Cut sequins in half and pull out.
- Avoid steam when working with beaded, sequin or metallic fabrics.

Fabrics with pile

- Trim the pile from the seam allowance to reduce bulk. To hide seams in furs, working from the right side, use a pin to pick out the pile from the seam stitching.
- When pressing fabrics with a pile or heavy texture, use a soft towel as a pressing surface or velvet board.

Sheer, fancy fabrics

- On transparent, sheer and lacy fabrics, use French seams, double-stitched or rolled hems, which look good on both sides of the fabric. Alternatively, bind seams and hems with a fine bias tape or lace edging.
- Use a small hole throat plate when sewing very fine fabrics to prevent the fabric being pulled into the throat plate.

Stretch fabrics

- For close-fitting knit garments, cut the pattern pieces slightly smaller than the actual size.
- Use zigzag or stretch stitches to sew knit fabrics.
- To prevent knit fabric edges curling, stitch a double row of stitching and trim close to the outer row.
- Stay stitch or edge tape any areas that are not supposed to stretch, such as the neck, armhole and shoulder seams.

FABRIC WIDTHS							
90 cm metre	36 in yard	115 cm metre	45 in yard	140 cm metre	54 in yard	150 cm metre	60 in yard
1.60	1¾	1.30	1⅜	1.05	1⅛	0.95	1
1.85	2	1.50	1⅝	1.30	1⅜	1.15	1¼
2.10	2¼	1.60	1¾	1.50	1½	1.30	1⅜
2.30	2½	1.95	2⅛	1.60	1¾	1.50	1⅝
2.65	2⅞	2.10	2¼	1.75	1⅞	1.60	1¾
2.90	3⅛	2.30	2½	1.85	2	1.75	1⅞
3.10	3⅜	2.55	2¾	2.10	2¼	1.85	2
3.45	3¾	2.65	2⅞	2.20	2⅜	2.10	2¼
3.90	4¼	2.90	3⅛	2.40	2⅝	2.20	2⅜
4.15	4½	3.10	3⅜	2.55	2¾	2.40	2⅝
4.35	4¾	3.35	3⅝	2.65	2⅞	2.55	2¾
4.60	5	3.55	3⅞	2.90	3⅛	2.65	2⅞

Fabric requirements

To determine the amount of fabric required when the fabric width of your chosen fabric differs from the pattern guidelines, use the chart above. Note that one-way designs, checks and stripes may need more fabric than the recommended amount. For example, if a pattern calls for 1.60 m (1¾ yd) of 115 cm (45 in) wide fabric, and your chosen fabric is 90 cm (36 in) wide, go to the 115 cm column, look down until you get to 1.60 m and then move along the row until you get to the 90 cm column. The amount of fabric required at the different width will be noted in this column, i.e. 2.10 m (2¼ yd).

Threads and notions

The choice of threads, notions and cutting equipment available nowadays means there is a tool for every task, many of which also make the job easier.

Threads

As well as general-purpose sewing threads, there are a number of specialist threads and natural fibre threads, all of which are available in a wide range of colours.

General-purpose threads – Nowadays most general-purpose threads are polyester-covered cottons which have the flexibility of polyester with the strength of cotton. This type of thread is perfectly acceptable for most general sewing projects. You will also find 100% polyester threads, which are stronger.

Silk threads – These are very soft and have a sheen, making them ideal for hand sewing or top stitching.

Machine embroidery – These are slightly finer than general-purpose threads because they are often used in highly concentrated stitch patterns. Most have a high gloss. They are often 100% polyester or rayon. There is a huge variety of threads, ranging from plain vibrant colours to metallics, variegated and iridescent. Use with a machine embroidery needle that has a larger eye suitable for highly dense stitching, which will also help prevent the thread splitting or breaking.

Bobbin fill – Designed for use with machine embroidery, this is a finer black or white thread used in the bobbin, and thus forming the underside of heavily stitched embroideries. Because it is finer, it decreases the density of the stitching on the reverse of the work, which helps prevent puckering.

EMBROIDERY THREADS

METALLIC THREADS

Metallic threads – Used for decorative stitching either by hand or machine. If machining, use with a metallic needle which has a coated eye because the metallic fibres can cut a minute groove in the eye, causing threads to shred and snap. Use thicker, uneven metallic threads on the bobbin rather than as the upper thread. Sew with the work facing downward to ensure the decorative thread is on the right side.

GENERAL-PURPOSE THREADS

SPECIALITY THREADS

Top stitch/buttonhole thread – Designed to be highly visible, this is a thicker thread, most often polyester. It is used for top stitching, decorative stitches or hand sewing buttons etc. Use a general-purpose thread in the bobbin and a jeans needle or machine embroidery needle with a larger eye to accommodate the thicker thread.

Quilting thread – This thread has a wax finish to help prevent tangling when hand stitching. A polycotton mix or 100% cotton, it can also be used for machine stitching.

Basting thread – Usually 100% cotton, basting thread is finer and rougher than general thread. It will break easily and is only used for temporarily holding fabrics together.

Invisible/transparent thread – Available in clear or smoke colour, it is a nylon thread designed for attaching trims, quilting and repairs.

Helpful hint: When choosing thread, hold a piece of fabric against the reel. If a perfect match isn't possible, choose a slightly darker shade as it will look lighter when unravelled off the reel.

Hand sewing threads

In addition to the machine threads which can be used for hand sewing, there are different, thicker threads used for embroidery, cross stitch, crochet, crewel and stumpwork. They are available in an extensive range of colours and varieties, on skeins, braids or spools and may be a mix of fibres or 100% cotton.

Mercerised or Perlé crochet thread – Used for cross stitch or crochet, it is usually 100% cotton and has a slight lustre.

Stranded cotton/embroidery floss – As the name suggests, these are made up of strands which can be separated and

Serging threads

As sergers (overlockers) use far more thread than a conventional sewing machine, specially designed threads come on larger cones, cops and reels (also known as bobbins). There are different qualities, each used for slightly different finishes. However, sewing machine decorative threads can be used in the loopers (which have larger eyed needles).

100% spun polyester/cotton wrapped polyester – Used in the needles, these threads are similar to sewing machine threads but finer.

Woolly nylon/floss – As the name suggests, this has a flossy/woolly texture with a slight sheen. It is used in the upper looper so that the soft wool is on the upper edge of the seam and is ideal for swimwear, fabrics with Lycra

EMBROIDERY FLOSSES

used separately or in combinations of 1–6, depending on the thickness required, to form stitches. Varieties include high sheen, matt finish, variegated in silks, cotton, linen or mixed fibres.

SERGER CONES

and lingerie. Bulk thread is similar without the sheen. It is good for stretch and knit fabrics.

Decorative threads – Conventional decorative threads can be used in the loopers which have larger eyed needles.

Cutting tools

There are all types of scissors, designed to make the cutting task easier. A good basic selection will include dressmaking shears, pinking shears, embroidery scissors, general-purpose scissors and a scissor sharpener.

Shears – These have moulded handles, with a smaller hole for the thumb and a larger one for the fingers. They are shaped for right or left hand use. Blades are long and straight for smooth long cuts. Handles may be angled from the blades so the blades sit parallel with the cutting surface and fabric remains flat. Some dressmaking shears have very fine serrated blades on the cutting edge which grip slippery fabric whilst cutting.

Pinking shears – As with dressmaking shears, these have shaped handles. The blades have a pronounced zigzag cutting edge that 'pink' fabrics to neaten raw edges. Use for neatening cottons, craft fabrics and other non-fray fabrics.

General-purpose scissors – Similar to shears, but the scissor handles have the same size apertures for fingers and thumb and can be used right- or left-handed. Some shears and scissors have soft touch handles, and a spongy surface within the grip area that makes handling and prolonged cutting easier on the hand. Spring touch scissors have handles one on top of the other and are designed for single hand use.

Needlework/embroidery scissors – Small scissors are convenient for snipping and clipping into tight curves and around notches etc. Those with curved tips are particularly useful for snipping threads close to machine embroidery work.

Sharpeners – Designed to remove burrs and nicks in scissor blades, these handy gadgets also keep scissors sharp for longer. However, they cannot be used with serrated blade or pinking shears.

Seam ripper – Also known as a quick-unpick, this is a useful tool for removing unwanted stitches quickly. Simply slip the blade under the stitch and slice through, repeating every 2.5–5 cm (1–2 in).

Rotary cutters – Used in conjunction with a ruler and self-healing cutting mat, rotary cutters are used to cut long straight lengths of fabric quickly and easily. Some cutters have retractable blades or blades with different cutting edges. They are usually very sharp so care should be taken when using them. They are ideal for patchwork and quilting, cutting bias strips and fabric for soft furnishings.

SHEARS AND GENERAL-PURPOSE SCISSORS

EMBROIDERY SCISSORS

SEAM RIPPER AND SCISSOR SHARPENER

Helpful hint: Use a seam ripper to open buttonholes neatly – push a pin through the fabric at one end, and slice with the ripper from the other end, working towards the pin.

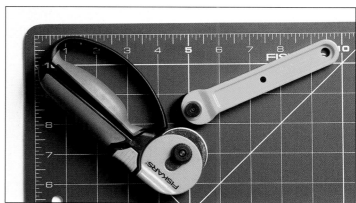
ROTARY CUTTER AND MAT

Marking tools

A number of different types of marking tool are available, used to transfer pattern matching notes from the tissue pattern to the fabric. Whenever possible mark the reverse of the fabric.

Chalk – Easily removed after use, chalk markers are quick and easy to use. Available in a variety of shapes and colours, there are chalk wheels, chalk pencils and chalk blocks. Chalk wheels work in one direction only and leave a fine trail of powder. Blocks can be used in any direction and leave a heavier line whilst chalk pencils are used in the same way as ordinary pencils.

Helpful hint: To mark darts – snip a hole in the tissue at the dart placement mark and use chalk to mark the spot. Pin through the fabric layers at this spot and, turning the layers over, make a chalk mark on the underside at the same point.

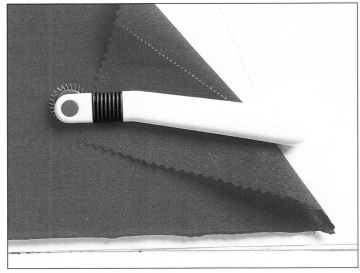

CARBON PAPER AND TRACING WHEEL

Marker pens – Some of the different types available include water-soluble, fadeaway and permanent. They are used in the same way as a normal pen. Vanishing or fadeaway pens and pencils are also known as evaporating or air-soluble pens. Marks simply fade away after about 48 hours. Water-soluble pens are usually blue. The mark can be removed later by sponging or washing.

Dressmaker's carbon paper and tracing wheel – A traditional marking tool, carbon papers are now available in a range of colours. There are also vanishing carbons. They can be used to mark two fabric layers at the same time by placing a folded sheet between fabric layers. As with all markings, use on the reverse of the fabric.

Needles

There is a huge variety of needles for both hand and machine sewing, with a selection of general-purpose needles and those designed for very specific jobs. Below is a list of the most common needles.

Hand needles

The length, point type, size of eye and shape of needle depends on the task for which it is designed. For instance, tapestry needles have blunt points and upholstery needles are curved so that they can be inserted and come out on the same side (essential when you can't get to the back of the work).

Mixed hand needles – Essential in every household, mixed hand needles provide a selection of different length and eye size needles to cope with general sewing repairs.

Ball point needles – Used when sewing knit and stretch fabrics, these have a rounded point which parts rather than pierces the fabric fibres.

Beading needles – These are used for adding beads by hand and are often curved. They are very fine with a small flat eye to go through small beads easily.

Helpful hint: Replace needles frequently because they will blunt over time and can snag delicate or knit fabrics, thereby spoiling the look of your work. For easy threading, cut thread at an angle.

CHALK MARKERS AND MARKER PENS

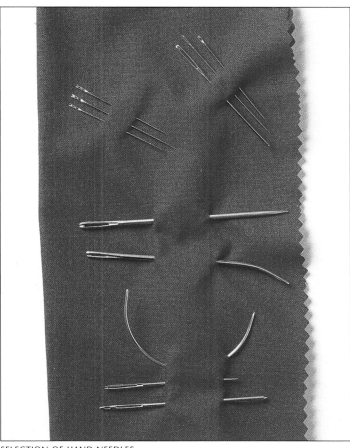

SELECTION OF HAND NEEDLES

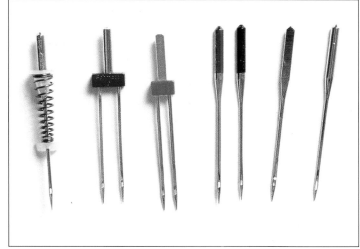

SELECTION OF MACHINE NEEDLES

Self-threading needles – Fairly new on the market and ideal for partially-sighted people, a split eye at the top makes threading a breeze.

Darning needles – These have a fairly blunt point and large eye to cope with heavier threads.

Upholstery needles – Some are curved, as mentioned above, and others have extra large eyes to take very thick threads or are extra long.

Bodkins – Used for threading elastic or ribbons through casings, a bodkin is not really a needle, but is shaped like one, with a rounded point and large flat eye.

Machine needles

As with hand needles, there are different machine needles for different types of fabric and techniques. Using the right needle will help ensure even, neat stitches.

One side of the needle shaft is flattened to ensure correct insertion into the needle aperture. Generally it is flat to back, but check your user's manual. Incorrect insertion can cause skipped stitches. Always tighten the needle in position using the screwdriver supplied in your sewing machine's tool kit otherwise it can work loose or move about when stitching.

Helpful hint: *For every new project, use a fresh needle. If using special needles for small amounts of sewing, paint the shaft with nail polish to colour code them.*

Helpful hint: *If a seam pulls up or stitches are skipped the needle may be too big; try a smaller size. If it breaks when stitching it may be too small; try a larger size.*

European sizes range from 60 to 120, while American sizes go from 9 to 20. Packs are usually numbered with both American and European sizing.

Use the following as a guide:

60–75 (9–11)
For lightweight fabrics such as chiffon, voiles, organza, silks and lingerie

80–90 (12–14)
For medium-weight fabrics and general dressmaking fabrics such as cottons, woollens and polyesters

100–110 (16–18)
For heavyweight fabrics and coatings such as heavy brocade, dense denim and canvas

120 (20)
For very heavyweight, thick and coarse fabrics

Common needle types

General-purpose, universal needles – Used for general sewing projects, they have a sharp point and come in different sizes to suit different fabric weights.

Sharps/microfibre needles – These have sharp points and are used for densely woven fabrics. Used for silks, buttonholes, top stitching.

Ball point needles – As with hand ball point needles, they have rounded tips to part the fibres as they stitch. Used for stretch knits, jerseys, fleece and velvet.

Embroidery/machine embroidery needles – These have a larger eye to cope with embroidery threads and novelty threads. Used with machine embroidery threads and for top stitching.

Metallic thread needles – Like embroidery needles, these have a larger eye, usually specially coated for extra protection against metallic threads that can wear away a small nick in the eye, causing the threads to break and shred. Used for metallic threads and machine embroidery.

Twin needles – Used to stitch two parallel rows of stitching at the same time, they have two needles on one shaft. Twin needles are available in universal, embroidery, stretch and ball point varieties. The distance between the needles can vary from 2–3 mm (¹⁄₁₆–¹⁄₈ in). Used for decorative top stitching and heirloom stitching.

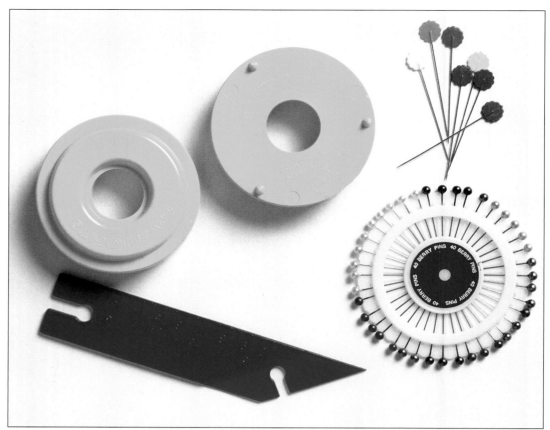

WEIGHTS, DRESSMAKING PINS AND A POINT TURNER

Jeans needles – These are sharply pointed strong needles, often with a blue top for easy recognition. Used for denim, heavy canvas, upholstery fabric, faux suede and top stitching.

Leather needles – To help penetrate leather, these needles have a triangular chisel point. Note: any stitches made will leave little holes so always test before stitching the main project. Used for leather, suede and faux suede.

Stretch needles – Designed with a 'scarf' to help pierce two-way stretch fabric. Used for swimwear, Lycra, rubber and lingerie.

Wing needles – These have a larger-shaped eye and are designed to leave little holes in the fabric as they stitch. Used for heirloom stitching.

Quilting needles – These have a longer, sharper point to penetrate several layers easily. Used for quilting.

Spring needles – These quite literally have a spring wrapped around the needle shaft. They can be used without a presser foot. Used for free motion embroidery.

Sergers (overlockers)

A variety of needles are also available for sergers, some of which are interchangeable with sewing machine needles. Check your user's manual.

Pins and weights

Pins are like needles and can blunt with repeated use. Change them regularly to prevent fabrics being snagged or laddered. Use weights (or tin cans) instead of pins when cutting out leather or fabrics that can be damaged by pin marks. Weights are also ideal when working on a large flat surface.

As with needles, there are a number of different types of pins to suit different fabrics and tasks. These range from sharp, universal, ball point, quilting, lace and upholstery pins. Dressmaking pins are

Helpful hint: Pin tissue to the fabric in the seam allowances, with pins parallel to the cutting line.

usually made from tempered, hardened steel. Some varieties have glass or plastic ball or flower heads which make removing and finding them easier. Take care when pressing, the plastic head can melt under a hot iron!

Pin basting – use instead of thread basting for quick and easy projects. Pin every 5–8 cm (2–3 in) on fine slippery fabrics; every 8–10 cm (3–4 in) on light- to medium-weight fabrics and 13–15 cm (5–6 in) on heavyweight fabrics. Increase the amount of pins at curves and when fitting two sections together such as sleeves into armholes or a skirt onto a waistband.

Handy accessories

As well as all the scissors, pins and needles and marking tools, there are a few other sewing aids that make life a little easier.

Point turner – Shaped to an angled point at one end, this useful tool also has measurements along one side. Used to push corners out fully on collars, cushion corners etc. They are also used for measuring hem allowances.

Rouleau turner – Long, thin and with a hook at one end, this device is used to turn fine tubing through to the right side.

Pressing tools

To achieve a professional finish to sewing projects, pressing accurately and often is essential. As well as a steam iron and press cloth, other useful pressing tools include the following:

Sleeve board – As the name suggests, this is a miniature ironing board used for ironing sleeves.

Seam roll – A well stuffed, sausage-shaped cloth roll, it is used to press over long straight seams without the underside being pressed at the same time – such as sleeves, shoulder yokes. A tightly rolled towel works just as well.

Tailor's ham – This is a stuffed, ham-shaped oval, hence the name. Use it to press open curved areas such as darts and princess seams.

Velvet/needle board – Used to press fabrics with a pile such as velvets, corduroy and fleece, it is a pad covered with fine steel needles. A soft fluffy towel works well as an alternative.

Pressing techniques

Pressing differs from ironing in that the iron is not moved back and forth, rather it is placed on the work, held for a moment, lifted and moved to the next position. This avoids fabrics being stretched as they are pressed.

- Press each seam as it is sewn and before being stitched over again.
- Press from the wrong side whenever possible using a press cloth.
- Before applying steam, test a fabric sample to see how it reacts.
- Leave work to cool fully before continuing.

SEAM ROLL AND TAILOR'S HAM

Interfacings and stabilizers

Interfacings are used to enhance the look of a garment, adding firmness and stability to specific areas such as collars, cuffs and front facings. Stabilizers are used to back fabric, holding it taut whilst stitching, particularly when doing machine embroidery.

Interfacings

There are many different types of interfacing, ranging from soft pliable ones to heavier, stiff canvas types for soft furnishings. Which to use depends on personal preference, the fabric being interfaced and the desired finish.

Generally, lightweight interfacings are used with lightweight fabrics. For very lightweight, transparent fabrics, an extra layer of the main fabric is sometimes used.

There are three main categories of interfacing, all of which come in fusible (iron-on) and sew-in varieties, in white, black and nude colours and in different weights.

Non-woven – Made from pressed fibres with a felt-like

SELECTION OF INTERFACINGS

appearance. Because there is no grain, they can be cut in any direction and pattern pieces placed any way up. Weights range from super light to extra heavy. Used for traditional home dressmaking and crafts.

Woven – These have a grain and are cut on the grain or bias in the same way as fabrics are. The super lightweights are ideal for silks, georgettes, sheers and satins. Medium- to heavyweight interfacings are used for jackets, dresses and blouses.

Knitted – These are made with a two-way stretch so they handle like knitted fabrics. Used for sportswear, knitted, stretch and pile fabrics.

Specialist interfacings

In addition to interfacings for general use, there are specialist versions for different sewing techniques including waistbanding, hemming, edge tape, craft and soft furnishing interfacings.

Waistbandings – Designed to be used in waistbands, front bands and pleats, they are non-woven and are usually fusible. Some have slotted lines to help fold and sew easily. Others have stiffened bands attached to the interfacing to provide roll-resistance in waistbands.

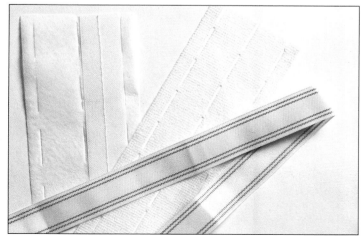

SELECTION OF WAISTBANDINGS

Hem tapes – Again, usually fusible, these are used to turn up hems without stitching. Hem web is a double-sided, very fine adhesive strip that melts, bonding the fabric when pressed. It is placed between the hem allowance and the main fabric. Bondahem is similar but has a paper backing so it can be applied in two stages or used to attach pockets etc. Blind hem tape is folded to mimic a sewn blind hem. Usually fusible, it is applied in the same way as hem webbing.

Bias tape – This is used to prevent unwanted stretch at necklines, armhole edges or any curve that needs stabilizing. It is a bias-cut fusible tape and is used within the seam allowance.

Edge tape – As with the bias tape, edge tape is used to add stability in areas that you don't want to stretch too much. It is a straight cut, narrow strip with reinforced stitching for added hold. It is very useful for adding firmness to areas which have been cut on the bias, such as shoulder seams and skirt slits.

SELECTION OF HEM TAPES

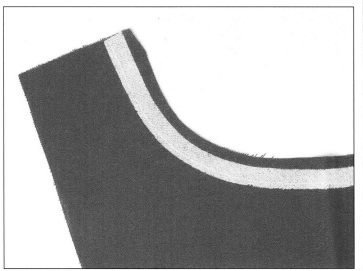
BIAS TAPE FUSED ONTO A CURVED AREA

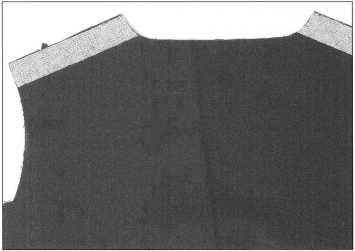
EDGE TAPE APPLIED TO A SHOULDER EDGE

Fleece, wadding or batting – This describes the soft interfacings that are used to add padding, bulk and warmth to quilts and other soft furnishings. Specialist versions include those made of compressed fleece which provides some heat resistance or those with pre-printed guide lines for quilting. Waddings and battings are described as having extra loft – otherwise known as bulk density.

Wadding comes in a variety of different weights, from lightweight (2 oz), to more heavyweight (12 oz). If you are making an item for a baby, such as a cot bumper, make sure that the wadding you are using conforms to safety standards.

Applying interfacings

Sew-in – Use sew-in on textured fabrics, those with pile, beading and sequins. Stitch the interfacing to the wrong side of the fabric piece just within the seam allowance and then trim close to the stitching so that there is none in the seam allowance. Trim the corners at an angle.

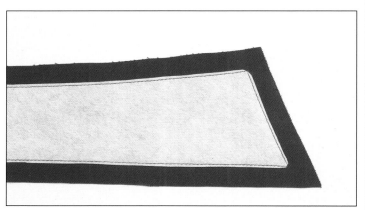

SEW-IN INTERFACING

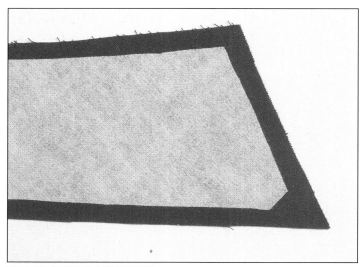

IRON-ON (FUSIBLE) INTERFACING

Iron-on (fusible) interfacing – Whilst very quick and easy to apply, iron-on interfacings and tapes must be fused properly to ensure they remain fixed, even when laundered. To apply, cut fusible interfacing to the size of the pattern piece then trim so it fits within the seam allowance. Fuse to the wrong side of the fabric, using a press cloth and dry iron. Press for approximately 10–15 seconds before lifting the iron and repositioning (do not slide the iron along as it might push the interfacing out of position). The actual time taken to fuse completely will differ between fabric and interfacing weights. Always test on a sample first. Allow to cool completely before continuing to work with the fabric.

Stabilizers

A stabilizer is used to back areas that are to be densely stitched, such as machine embroidery, buttonholes and appliqué. Varieties include tearaway, water-soluble, heat-off, self-adhesive and permanent stabilizers. Stabilizers help prevent fine fabrics being pulled down into the throat plate and the fabric puckering when stitched.

SELECTION OF STABILIZERS

Helpful hint: *Take care when pulling away tearaway stabilizer because you do not want to spoil your work.*

Tearaway – Crisp to handle with a flat felt-like finish, tearaway stabilizers are positioned on the reverse of the fabric, under the area to be stitched. After stitching, simply tear away the excess.

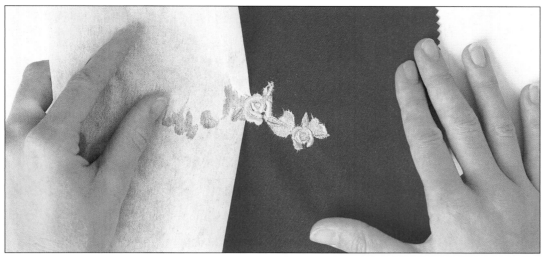

TEARAWAY STABILIZER

Self-adhesive embroidery backer – This is used to back small areas such as cap peaks, cuffs and collars. It has a layer of paper covering the adhesive side. Once hooped, the garment section can be adhered to the embroidery backer by removing the paper from the appropriate area.

Paper-backed fusible web – This is a double-sided fusible web, backed on one side with paper. It is ideal for applying appliqué. The designs to be appliquéd are drawn on the paper backing (in reverse) then cut out roughly. Position this on the wrong side of the fabric, web side to fabric, and fuse in place. Cut out accurately and then place in position, peeling the paper backing away. Again, press in place. Finish with satin stitch or zigzag stitch to seal the edges. Alternatively, use fabric paint.

Water-soluble – There are many types of water-soluble stabilizer, ranging from very fine, fabric-like qualities to heavy-duty films. They are used in areas that need stabilizing whilst being stitched, but which need to be removed afterwards. They can also be used on the front of work to prevent stitches disappearing into pile fabrics such as velvet and towelling. Use them in single or multiple layers, depending on the thickness of the pile. Very fine fabrics should be sandwiched between two layers of stabilizer.

Once the area has been stitched, wash away the stabilizer by soaking the work in cold water. The stabilizer will just dissolve away. Rinse well. Heat-off versions are removed by ironing the area – the stabilizer turns brown then crumbles away.

WATER-SOLUBLE STABILIZER

Helpful hint: *To create stitched sculptures, use the heavy-duty soluble stabilizer and wash gently until the desired crispness remains.*

PAPER-BACKED FUSIBLE WEB

Paper patterns

Paper patterns are readily available for all kinds of sewing, from dressmaking to crafts and soft furnishings. The majority of the commercial pattern brands use the same sizing code, pattern markings and terminology.

The pattern pack

Inside commercial patterns there are tissue sheets on which are printed all the full size paper pattern pieces plus illustrated step-by-step construction notes. On the envelope itself are photographs or illustrations of the garments or projects included in the pack, line drawings showing details such as zippers, buttons and darts, a list and quantity guide for all materials and notions required, suggested fabrics and a table of sizes and measurements.

Pattern sizing – Shown on the envelope are the main measurements – bust, waist, hip, back length. Check these against your own personal measurements to determine your pattern size Note: it may not be the same as your ready-to-wear size. If you are different sizing for top and bottoms, use your hip measurement for trousers and skirts and your bust measurement for tops, jackets and dresses.

Garment sizes – These may be listed on the envelope or on the tissue pieces. They will give the measurements of the finished garment, which will include wearing ease and designer ease and thus can be considerably bigger than your personal body measurements.

Suggested fabrics – This section includes a list of suitable fabrics. Whilst other fabrics can be used, only those recommended have been tested. In particular, avoid using checks and stripes unless listed.

Fabric requirements – Noted on the reverse of the envelope, the list includes requirements for different fabric widths and sizes. It will also include 'with nap' and 'without nap' requirements. Follow with nap quantities when working with pile, novelty or fabrics with sheen.

Tissue pattern – Many dressmaking patterns are multi-size and thus have cutting lines for each size around each piece. There may also be a choice of notch and dart positions. Follow the lines that correspond to your size. Most international patterns include seam allowances within the pattern pieces, which are generally 1.5 cm (⅝ in).

Sizing

In commercial patterns an average woman is categorized as 'Misses', and is 165–168 cm (5 ft 5 in–5 ft 6 in) tall with a B cup size (see the measurements charts on page 37). Women or Women Plus patterns are for those with fuller figures whilst teen designs are categorized as Junior/Teen, and children's patterns are sized by age and average measurements.

The wearing ease, mentioned earlier, is the amount of 'wriggle' room that has been incorporated. Therefore a coat that is designed to wear over a jacket will have ample room, whilst a boned bodice will have very little. In addition, there might be 'designer' ease, built in by the designer to create the style envisaged.

Pattern terminology

In addition to sizing, the terminology used by pattern companies is fairly universal. Pattern instructions and pattern pieces have various markings to help with fitting together, lengthening, shortening and shaping.

1 Pattern number, section, number of pieces to be cut.
2 Notches – matched evenly side to side, back to front etc. Cut notches outward into fabric.
3 Multi-size cutting lines – follow the line for your size. When lines converge, follow the single line.
4 Circles – used as placement marks for pockets etc. or to indicate where to stop and start stitching. Transfer to the fabric with a marking pen, chalk or tailor's tacks (see Hand stitching, page 41).
5 Lengthen/shorten line – adjust length at this point. Fold pattern up to shorten by the required amount, or cut through the tissue and separate by the required amount to lengthen.
6 Darts – transfer the markings from the tissue to the fabric. Darts are used to shape garments. On multi-size patterns, follow the darts for your size only.

7 Grain line – this line should run perfectly parallel with the selvage. Measure from the line to the selvage at either end to ensure it is accurate.

8 Fold line – place the pattern piece on the fold of the fabric so that when cut out the piece is double the size and symmetrical. Fold the fabric right sides together, with the selvages parallel.

9 Pleats, tucks and buttonholes – these lines indicate where to take or make pleats, tucks and buttonholes. Transfer to the fabric as with circles and darts.

Other sewing terminology, used frequently in construction notes includes the following:

Selvage – The bound side edges of the fabric.

Grain – The direction of the weave on woven fabrics. The lengthwise or straight grain runs parallel with the selvages. The crosswise grain runs from selvage to selvage and the bias is a diagonal; true bias is at a 45-degree angle from the lengthwise grain.

Nap – Indicates a fabric with a pile, sheen or textural surface that goes one way. All pieces cut from nap fabric must be cut facing the same way to prevent uneven shading. Use 'with nap' layouts for checks, plaids and any patterned fabric with a one-way design. If possible, use with the nap running downward. With nap layouts usually require more fabric than those without.

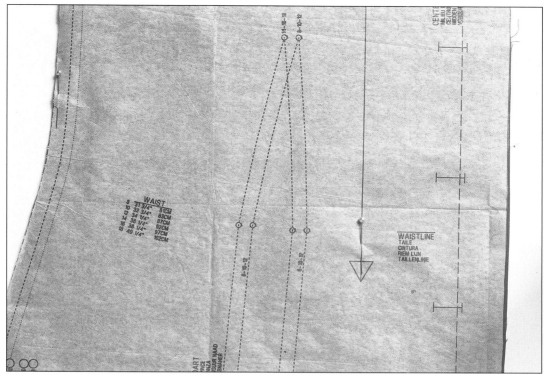

PATTERN PIECE WITH MARKINGS

Notching and clipping – These terms describe how to treat curved seams to ensure they lay flat. Notching is cutting wedge-shaped triangles from the seam allowance on outer curves. Clip into the seam allowance of inner curves, cutting close to stitching every 2.5–3 cm (1½ in) (diagram 1).

Grading seams – Used to reduce the bulk of fabric within the seams on heavier fabrics. The two seam allowances of each layer of fabric are cut a different width. Cut the under seam allowance to a minimal 3 mm (⅛ in) and the top seam allowance that will lie closest to the outer fabric 6 mm (¼ in) (diagram 2).

DIAGRAM 1

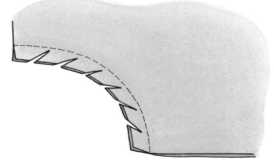

DIAGRAM 2

Fabric layouts

Fabric layouts showing how to place pattern pieces on fabric are provided for each of the views included in the pattern. There will be layouts for different fabric widths, with and without nap. All the pattern pieces needed for each view are also noted next to the layout which also shows whether to cut pieces from single or double layers of fabric (diagram 3).

DIAGRAM 3

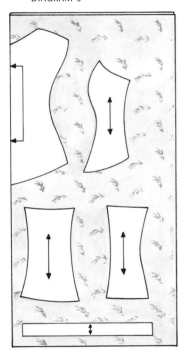

Helpful hint: To ensure you follow the correct layout, highlight which to use with a marker pen.

Pattern alterations

Nowadays most commercial patterns are multi-sized with three or more sizes printed on the tissue paper for each piece. The sizes differs at crucial fitting points, such as neck, bust, waist, hip and crotch as well as being slightly smaller or bigger in width, whilst at other areas, the size lines converge. Unfortunately it is not a matter of simply increasing a pattern piece by the same amount all around. Pattern alterations are also needed to suit individual figure varations such as for a larger fuller bust, fuller upper arms, higher or lower bottom, wider hips or a thicker waist.

The following are basic alterations only. Check the fit by tissue fitting or making a sample garment in calico before cutting out fashion fabrics. Remember to alter all corresponding pattern pieces, i.e. front, back and facings.
Lengthening or shortening – For minimal differences, adjust at the hemline. However, for more than 3 cm (1¼ in) use the lengthen/shorten line on the pattern tissue, which is placed to ensure the style isn't spoilt when the garment length is altered. On patterns without lengthen lines:
• Back neck to waist length – alter midway between the bust and the waist. Redraw any darts that are affected.
• Waist to hem – alter between the hip and the hem (if not altering at hemline).
• A-line dress and skirt – alter below the hipline.
• Sleeves – alter partway down the sleeve.

DIAGRAM 4

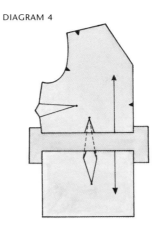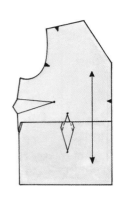

• Trousers/shorts – to increase/decrease the crotch depth, alter below the darts but above the crotchline.

To lengthen, cut the pattern piece across the width and spread apart by the desired amount. Add extra tissue in the gap and tape together. Redraw any darts or princess seaming. To shorten, fold tissue paper across the width by the desired amount. Tape in position. Again redraw darts if necessary (diagram 4).
Darts – Used to add shape to flat fabric, these can be increased in size, decreased, added or left out completely in order to shape more or less of the fabric to fit over fuller busts, rounded or flat bottoms etc. For example, people with flat bottoms require thin short darts and minimal shaping, whilst those with fuller bottoms require deeper, curved darts. The same applies for tummies.

• Bust darts should apex just before the fullest point of the bust. Pin out the dart on the tissue paper and check the position against your body – if it is not in the right place, mark your apex on the tissue then redraw the dart stitching lines from the new point to the original base at the seam line (diagram 5).

DIAGRAM 5

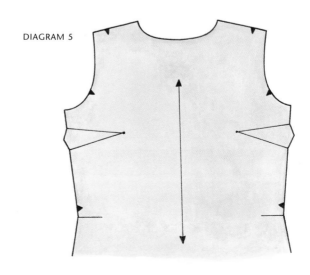

- Waist darts are used to shape and fit fabric through the torso. These can be increased or decreased to take in more or less fabric. Waist darts also need shortening if bust darts are lowered so that darts are not too close. Simply shorten the waist darts so the distance between the apex of the bust and the top of the waist dart remains the same as before the alterations (diagram 6).

DIAGRAM 6

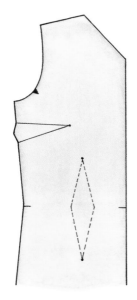

Transferring and enlarging patterns

Always pre-wash and press the fabric before cutting, particularly when adding linings (which might otherwise shrink at different levels).

The pattern templates provided for the projects in this book are in UK sizes 10, 12 and 14 (equivalent to US sizes 8, 10 and 12). Enlarge the templates by the percentage given, or copy onto 1 cm (⅜ in) squared dressmaker's pattern drafting paper. The following measurements are for guidance only.

Helpful hint: All darts should be pressed over a ham or curve to create the shape in the fabric (see below).

SIZE GUIDE	centimetres	inches
Size 10 (UK) Size 8 (US)		
Bust	83.0	32½
Waist	64.0	25
Hip	88.0	34½
Nape of neck to waist	40.5	16
Size 12 (UK) Size 10 (US)		
Bust	87.0	34
Waist	67.0	26½
Hips (23 cm/9 in below waist)	92.0	36
Nape of neck to waist	41.5	16¼
Size 14 (UK) Size 12 (US)		
Bust	92.0	36
Waist	71.0	28
Hip	97.0	38
Nape of neck to waist	42.0	16½

General tips

- All seam allowances have been included in the patterns and measure 1.5 cm (⅝ in) unless otherwise stated.
- Cut out around the notches and transfer all other pattern markings to the fabric.
- Fold the fabric right sides together unless otherwise stated, folded lengthwise with selvages together. When the pattern is cut on folded fabric, there will be a right and left piece cut at the same time.
- When cutting a bias-cut garment, work with a single layer of fabric. Remember, to get a right- and left-hand section, it is then necessary to flip the pattern over.
- Place the pattern on the fabric right side up unless otherwise stated.
- Place all pattern pieces with the straight of grain line in the same direction i.e. top to bottom.
- The grain line on the pattern tissue (straight line in centre of tissue piece) should run parallel to the selvage.
- To increase the size above UK size 14 (US size 12), the difference between tissue size and own measurements has to be divided by the number of pieces. Therefore if there are two front pieces and two back pieces, divide the difference by 4 so that a little is added to each piece at the side seam.
- Cut out and make up a calico sample if you are unsure of the sizing – this will avoid costly mistakes.
- Use notches to match side seams etc. Use circular or triangular points to match placement for pockets and folds for darts and pleats.
- Read all pattern instructions before starting.

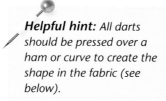

DART BEING PRESSED OVER A HAM

Measuring guide

Before deciding which commercial pattern size you need to make, it is first necessary to take some basic body measurements. Wear your usual underwear and, standing barefoot, take bust, waist, hip, high bust and back neck to waist measurements.

Bust – Measure around the fullest part of the bust and straight across the back. The tape should remain parallel to the floor.

High bust – This is directly under the arms and above the bust and straight across the back.

Waist – To find the natural waistline tie a string around the waist and bend side to side. It will roll into the crease that forms at the natural waistline.

Hips – Measure at the fullest part – approximately 18–23 cm (7–9 in) below waist (diagram 1).

DIAGRAM 1

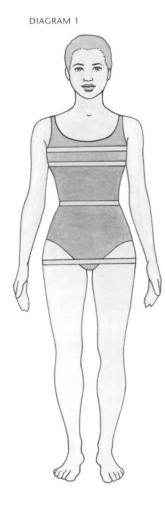

DIAGRAM 2

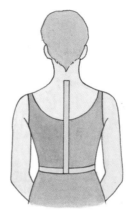

DIAGRAM 3

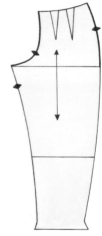

Helpful hints:
• *If you are making skirts, trousers and shorts, use the hip measurement to determine the pattern size.*
• *If you are making jackets, tops and dresses, use the bust measurement to determine the pattern size.*
• *If the difference between the bust and the high bust measurement is more than 6.5 cm (2½ in), select the pattern size by the high bust measurement.*

Other useful measurements include:
Back waist length – From the base of the neck (most prominent bone) to the natural waistline (diagram 2).
Bust point – Measure from the base of the neck/shoulder to the fullest point of the bust. On a paper pattern check this measurement (remember to allow for seam allowances), it should be 2.5 cm (1 in) from the dart point.
Shoulder length – From the base of the neck to the shoulder edge. If it is broader or narrower than the pattern piece, adjustments to the pattern will need to be made.

Crotch length – Measure from the waistline at the back, down through the legs to the waistline at the front. Divide the measurement into front and back crotch lengths at the mid-point between the legs. Check the measurements against the tissue pattern crotch line. If the pattern needs to be altered, make alterations below the dart and above the crotch.
Crotch depth – Sit on a hard chair to take the measurement from the waistline to the seat down the outside leg seam line. Check the measurement against the pattern as above (diagram 3).

METRIC
Misses'/Miss Petite – For well-proportioned, developed figures.
Misses' about 165–168 cm without shoes. Miss Petite under 163 cm without shoes.

Sizes	4 /US 2	6/US 4	8/US 6	10/US 8	12/US 10	14/US 12	16/US 14	18/US 16	20/US 18	22/US 20	24/US 22	26/US 24	
Sizes – European	30	32	34	36	38	40	42	44	46	48	50	52	
Bust	75	78	80	83	87	92	97	102	107	112	117	122	cm
Waist	56	58	61	64	67	71	76	81	87	94	99	106	cm
Hip – 23 cm below waist	80	83	85	88	92	97	102	107	112	117	122	127	cm
Back waist length	38.5	39.5	40	40.5	41.5	42	42.5	43	44	44	44.5	44.5	cm
Petite – back waist length	36	37	37.5	38	38.5	39.5	40	40.5	41.5	41.4	42	42	cm

Women's/Women's Petite – For the larger, more fully mature figures.
Women's about 165–168 cm without shoes. Women's Petite under 163 cm without shoes.

Sizes	18W/US 16	20W/US 18	22W/US 20	24W/US 22	26W/US 24	28W/US26	30W/US 28	32W/US 30	
Sizes – European	44	46	48	50	52	54	56	58	
Bust	102	107	112	117	122	127	132	137	cm
Waist	84	89	94	99	105	112	118	124	cm
Hip – 23 cm below waist	107	112	117	122	127	132	137	142	cm
Back waist length	43	44	44	44.5	45	45	45.5	46	cm
Petite – back waist length	40.5	41.5	41.5	42	42	42.5	42.5	43	cm

Unisex – For figures within Misses', Men's, Teen-Boys', Boys' and Girls' size ranges.

Sizes	XXS	XS	S	M	L	XL	XXL	
Bust	71-74	76-81	87-92	97-102	107-112	117-122	127-132	cm
Waist	74-76	79-83	89-94	99-104	109-114	119-124	130-135	cm

IMPERIAL
Misses'/Miss Petite – For well-proportioned, developed figures.
Misses' about 5′ 5″ to 5′ 6″ without shoes. Miss Petite under 5′ 4″ without shoes.

Sizes	4/US 2	6/US 4	8/US 6	10/US 8	12/US 10	14/US 12	16/US 14	18/US 16	20/US 18	22/US 20	24/US 22	26 /US 24	
Sizes – European	30	32	34	36	38	40	42	44	46	48	50	52	
Bust	29½	30½	31½	32½	34	36	38	40	42	44	46	48	in
Waist	22	23	24	25	26½	28	30	32	34	37	38	41½	in
Hip – 9 in below waist	31½	32½	33½	34½	36	38	40	42	44	46	48	50	in
Back waist length	15½	15½	15¾	16	16¼	16½	16¾	17	17¼	17⅜	17½	17¾	in
Petite – back waist length	14¼	14½	14¾	15	15¼	15½	15¾	16	16¼	16⅜	16½	16⅝	in

Women's/Women's Petite – For the larger, more fully mature figures.
Women's about 5′ 5″ to 5′ 6″ without shoes. Women's Petite under 5′ 4″ without shoes.

Sizes	18W/US 16	20W/US 18	22W/US 20	24W/US 22	26W/US 24	28W/US 26	30W/US 28	32W /US 30	
Sizes – European	44	46	48	50	52	54	56	58	
Bust	40	42	44	46	48	50	52	54	in
Waist	33	35	37	39	41½	44	46½	49	in
Hip – 9 in below waist	42	44	46	48	50	52	54	56	in
Back waist length	17⅛	17¼	17⅜	17½	17⅝	17¾	17⅞	18	in
Petite – back waist length	16⅛	16¼	16⅜	16½	16⅝	16¾	16⅞	17	in

Unisex – For figures within Misses', Men's, Teen-Boys', Boys' and Girls' size ranges.

Sizes	XXS	XS	S	M	L	XL	XXL	
Chest/Bust	28-29	30-32	34-36	38-40	42-44	46-48	50-52	in
Hip	29-30	31-32½	35-37	39-41	43-45	47-49	51-53	in

Basic techniques

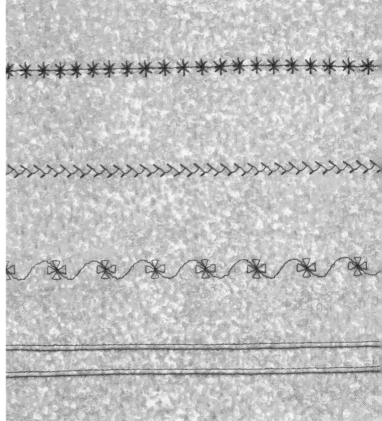

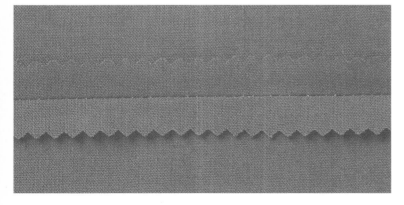

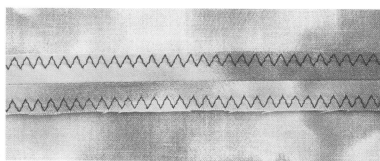

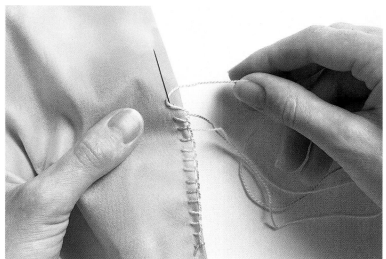

Hand stitching

Nowadays most hand stitching is used to mend, hem, apply badges and prepare or finish off garments, unless you are using embroidery or cross stitch creatively. The basic stitches needed are therefore basting or gathering, tailor's tacks, slip stitch, back and running stitch, blanket stitch and blind hem stitch.

Running stitch

The most common hand stitch, it is used to hold fabric layers together and has neat even stitches, approximately 3 mm (⅛ in) long with even gaps in between. Use general-purpose thread, approximately 40 cm (16 in) long. Secure the thread at one end with a knot or by taking 3–4 tiny stitches on the spot. Starting at the front of the work, pass the needle from front to back, then up to the front again in one pass. For speed, weave the needle in and out of the fabric 3–4 times in one go (diagram 1).

DIAGRAM 1

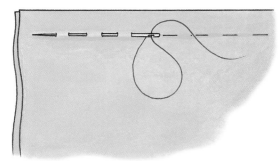

Gathering stitch

This is the same as running stitch, but with slightly longer stitches, 6–13 mm (¼–½ in). It is used to pull up fabric into gathers or to attach a longer piece of fabric to a shorter piece. Use doubled thread for strength. Once stitched, pull up the thread to gather the fabric, adjust the folds and gathers evenly and then stitch 3–4 times on the spot to hold in place (diagram 2).

Helpful hint: *When gathering long sections prevent the thread breaking or uneven gathering by separating the length into two or three sections and gather each separately.*

DIAGRAM 2

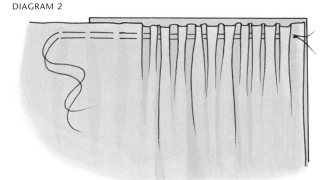

Basting

Also known as tacking, basting is used to temporarily hold together two or more layers of fabric. There are two methods: pin basting (see Threads and notions, page 27) and thread basting, which can be by machine or hand. Hand basting is the same process as running stitch, using basting or general-purpose thread approximately 46 cm (18 in) long with knotted end and large 13 mm (½ in) stitches which will be removed later. (To remove, cut off the knot, then cut the thread at intervals and pull out. Remove before pressing.) To machine baste, set the sewing machine to the longest stitch length possible and stitch within the seam allowance.

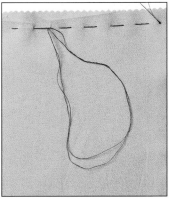

HAND BASTING FABRIC LAYERS

Helpful hint: *When basting, use a contrasting colour thread that is easy to see and therefore to remove after stitching.*

Tailor's tacks

Traditionally used to mark placement points on fabric for pockets, zippers, darts, pleats etc, they consist of 3–4 large loopy hand stitches made through all layers, then carefully cut so that thread remains in each layer. To make a tailor's tack, use general-purpose thread, doubled.

• With tissue paper uppermost, take a stitch through the placement mark, through all layers, leaving a large loop of thread at the back and the thread tail at the front. Repeat three times. Cut off the thread, leaving the thread tail again.

• Unpin the tissue and snip through the loops on both sides, then carefully pull the fabric layers apart and snip the threads again so that the thread remains in both fabric layers.

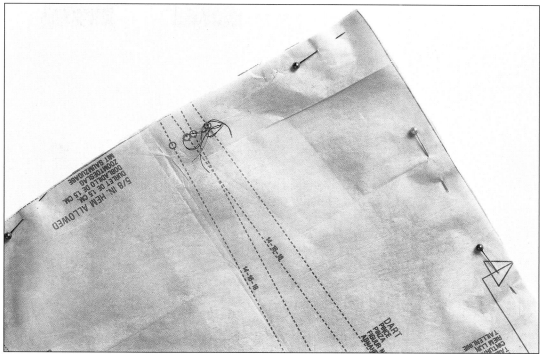
COMPLETED TAILOR'S TACK

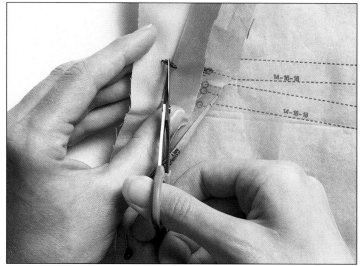
SNIPPING BETWEEN THE FABRIC LAYERS

Helpful hint: *Use a contrasting coloured thread to denote different placement points, for example, blue for zipper placement, red for pleats.*

Back stitch

Similar to straight stitching by machine, back stitch by hand is the strongest of the hand seaming stitches as the stitches at the front of the work are close together and at the back they overlap slightly. As before, start with 3–4 stitches on the spot or a knot, then take a small backward stitch from front to back and up to front 3 mm (⅛ in) in front, all in one pass. For the next and subsequent stitches, stitch backward again, inserting the needle through to the back at the end of the first stitch, and up again 3 mm (⅛ in) in front (diagram 3).

DIAGRAM 3

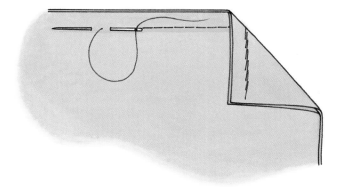

DIAGRAM 4

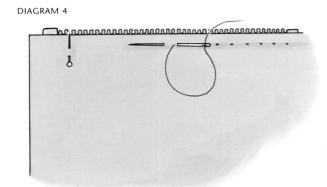

Prick stitch

Similar to back stitch, the stitches taken are tiny in order to be virtually invisible. Prick stitch is used on fabrics with a delicate texture or pile that might be spoiled with machine stitching. On the right side, the stitches are tiny and evenly spaced whilst on the reverse they resemble back stitch. As with back stitch, secure the thread then take a backward stitch from front to back and up to front a very scant 2–3 mm (¹⁄₁₆–⅛ in) ahead. Go back to reverse just 2–3 fibres behind the first stitch and repeat (diagram 4).

DIAGRAM 5

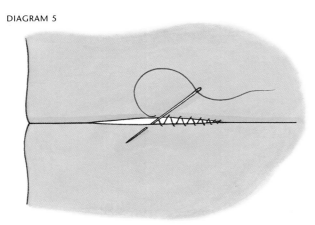

Slip stitch

Used to close gaps left to turn work to the right side or as a hemming technique, slip stitch is another stitch that should be virtually invisible. Use a thread to closely match the trim or fabric being stitched. Working from right to left, secure the thread then pull the needle through one folded edge, then a stitch of the same size through the other folded edge. Work along the gap, bringing the sides together (diagram 5). If hemming, take up just 1–2 fibres of the main fabric and a longer 6 mm (¼ in) stitch in the folded hem allowance.

WHIP STITCH

Whip stitch

This is a strong overedge stitch, usually used to attach trims to soft furnishings or badges and motifs to garments. Use thread to match the trim or motif. Having secured the thread under the trim, bring the needle from the back of the main fabric through to the front of the trim, take over the trim edge and through to the main fabric, picking up 2–3 fibres only. Bring back through the trim, over the edge to the main fabric again.

OVERCAST STITCH

Overcast stitch

Similar to whip stitch, overcast stitch is used to neaten raw edges. Bring the needle through from back to front of the fabric 3 mm (⅛ in) from the edge, then take over the edge to the back before coming through the fabric to the front again, a little to the left of the first stitch.

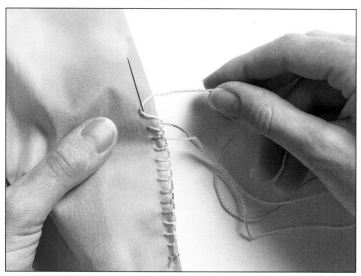

BLANKET STITCH

DIAGRAM 6

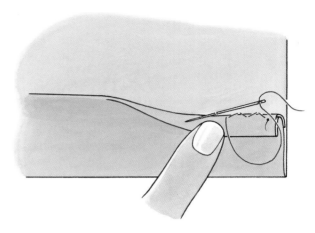

Blanket stitch

A decorative edge stitch used to finish the edges of blankets or throws on fabrics that do not fray, or to hold fabric edges together. On fabrics that fray, such as velvet, fold a double hem before blanket stitching over it. The stitch is often made using thicker thread or contrasting coloured threads. Wool or fine ribbon can also be used. Having secured the thread at the back of the work, bring the needle through from back to front, 6 mm (¼ in) from the edge. With the needle only part way through, loop the thread round the needle before pulling it all the way through, pushing the loop to sit on the fabric edge. Again, take the needle from back through to front approximately 6 mm (¼ in) further along, loop the thread over the needle and pull through again. Continue along the edge. At corners, work three stitches into the same hole.

Helpful hint: Draw a chalk stitching line 6 mm (¼ in) from the edge to keep the stitches even and neat.

Blind hem stitch

Hand stitched blind hemming should be invisible from the right side of the fabric. It is made by taking small stitches in the main fabric and larger stitches in the hem allowance, which has been folded back so that no stitching shows from either side. In order to maintain a soft rounded hem, avoid pressing the hem edge, just press the stitched area gently to embed the stitches.

- Fold the raw edge under at least 13 mm (½ in), then fold the hem allowance up and pin in position.
- Starting at one edge, secure the thread (colour matched to fabric) in the hem allowance and then in the top of the hem allowance back on itself, in order to take a stitch approximately 6 mm (¼ in) from the fold.
- Next pick up one or two fibres from the main fabric before taking up a longer stitch in the folded hem allowance, approximately 1 cm (⅜ in) along the hem (diagram 6).

Helpful hint: To ensure absolutely no stitching is seen on the outside of the garment, fuse edge tape to the main fabric under the hem allowance and pick up fibres from the tape rather than the main fabric.

Machine stitching

There are a number of functional machine stitches used in dressmaking and soft furnishings, mostly based on straight or zigzag stitch or a combination of both. These stitches are found on most sewing machines and are used for specific sewing techniques or finishes.

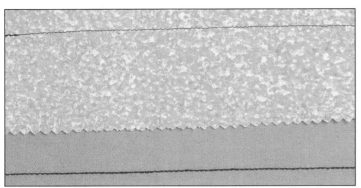

EXAMPLES OF STRAIGHT STITCH

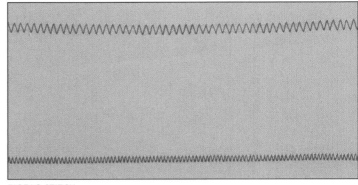

ZIGZAG STITCH

Straight stitch

As the name suggests, this is a straight line of stitching, most commonly used to sew seams and join fabric layers together. An average stitch length for a medium-weight fabric is 2.5 mm (10 stitches per inch). Increase the stitch length when stitching on heavier or bulky fabrics and reduce it to sew finer fabrics. The amount of adjustment will depend on the thickness and number of layers so always test on a sample piece of fabric of the same weight, number of layers and interfacing. If the seam starts to pucker, increase the stitch length slightly. If the fabric gathers easily and the stitches appear loose, reduce the stitch length slightly.

Reverse stitch

This is the same as straight stitch, but stitching backward. Usually achieved by holding down a button or lever on the sewing machine. It is used to fix stitching at the start and end of a seam. Zigzag stitch can also be stitched in reverse.

Helpful hint: To prevent threads tangling at the start of a seam, turn the balance wheel by hand until the needle comes back up with the bobbin thread looped with the top thread. Hold both thread tails behind the needle, start stitching about 2.5 cm (1 in) from the fabric edge, reverse to 1.5 cm (⅝ in) from the fabric edge then straight stitch again.

Zigzag stitch

This stitch has both width and length directions, both of which can be altered to increase or decrease the stitch width or length. Width is altered to reduce stitch size from side to side. Length is altered to reduce the distance between the stitches. Zigzag stitch is used to stitch a flexible seam on stretch fabrics or neaten raw edges. When neatening, stitch so the outer swing of the needle falls outside the raw edge.

Variations of straight stitch

Machine basting – As with hand basting, this is used to hold fabric layers together temporarily. Stitches are removed once the seam is sewn. Use a contrasting colour thread and do not fix stitch at the start or finish. Use the longest machine stitch length available and hold the fabric in front and behind the presser foot to prevent it gathering whilst being stitched. To remove basting, snip the basting stitches at intervals and then pull out the thread. Machine basting is useful when fitting skirts to waistbands, sleeves into armholes, collars onto neck edges etc.
Gathering stitch – This is the same as machine basting but with a slightly shorter stitch. Guide the fabric loosely, allowing the fabric to gather

as it is being stitched. Pull-up the bobbin thread to gather further before tying the thread ends in a knot to secure.

Stay stitch – This is a row or line of stitching just inside the seam allowance – 13 mm (½ in) from the raw edge. Use a regular stitch length. Stay stitching is used to prevent bias-cut edges and curves, necklines and shoulders from stretching too much whilst being handled.

Helpful hint: *Stay stitch in the same direction as the fabric grain, which can be determined by 'stroking the cat'. Run a finger along the cut edge: as a cat's fur is smooth one way when stroked, so the fibres of the fabric will curl smoothly one way.*

DIAGRAM 2

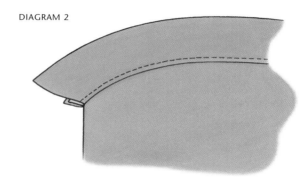

Ease stitch

This is similar to gathering stitch and stay stitch. Increase the stitch length to between 3–5 mm (⅛–¼ in), depending on the thickness of the fabric, and, if necessary, slightly loosen the needle tension so that the fabric gathers very, very slightly. Stitch within the seam allowance, close to the seam line. Ease stitch is used to fit slightly longer pieces of fabric to shorter lengths such as sleeves into sleeve heads without any gathers or folds appearing on the right side of the garment. Once stitched, match the notches and fit the eased section to the straight piece (diagram 1). If necessary, draw the bobbin thread of the ease stitching up slightly to improve the fit and distribute the fullness evenly. With the eased section uppermost, finish by machine stitching the pieces together.

Under stitch

A regular straight stitch, this is used on facings etc. to prevent them rolling to the outside. Before under stitching, seam allowances should be graded and clipped (see Paper patterns, page 33) and then pressed towards the facing. With the garment right side up and the facing held out, stitch through the facing and seam allowances, 3 mm (⅛ in) from the seam line. Fold the facing back inside and press with a press cloth (diagram 2).

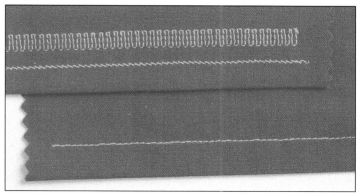
TOP STITCH

Top stitch

This is quite simply stitching on top of the fabric to provide a decorative finish or as a functional aid to attach patch pockets, machine stitch hems and keep facings and seam allowances flat. For straight rows, stitch with a slightly longer than usual stitch length (3–5 mm/⅛–¼ in), decreasing the length slightly when stitching around curves. If used for decorative purposes, use a contrasting coloured thread.

Helpful hint: *Use a stitching guide such as the edge of the fabric or the edge of the presser foot or mark a chalk line to ensure that the stitching remains an accurate distance from the edge.*

DIAGRAM 1

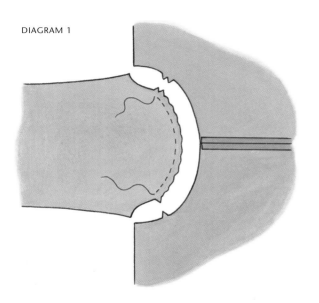

EDGE STITCH

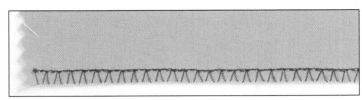

OVERCAST EDGE

Edge stitch

Edge stitch is an extra row of stitching on the right side of the fabric, designed to be visible. It is similar to top stitch (see page 45) but is usually stitched much closer to the fold, seam or finished edge (2–3 mm/⅛ in). It is usually stitched in matching thread. Edge stitching produces a crisp neat edge and helps prevent facings and seam allowances from rolling out. Press the edges to be stitched. To keep the stitching accurate, use a zipper or clear plastic foot with the needle to the far right so that the foot holds the fabric.

If you are a beginner or unsure of your stitching accuracy – leave it out.

Variations of zigzag stitch

Overcast – Using the zigzag stitch option, overcast stitch is used to neaten raw edges of fabric. Stitch with the fabric edge placed so the right swing of the needle falls off the fabric. For heavier fabrics, increase the stitch length and width and for lightweight fabrics, decrease the stitch width. If fabrics fray easily, overcast the fabric edges before stitching the seams.

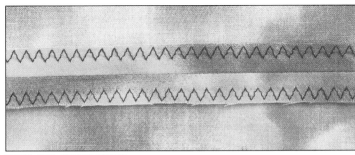

THREE-STEP ZIGZAG STITCH

Three-step zigzag stitch – Also known as tricot stitch, this is another zigzag stitch used to neaten edges. The zigzags are made in three stitches, hence the name. It provides a flatter finish than regular zigzag stitch. Stitch close to the raw edge of the trimmed seam (not overlapping).

DIAGRAM 3

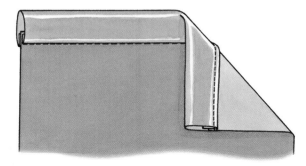

Stitch in the ditch

This is the term used to describe a line of straight stitching sewn within the seam in order to hold facings, casings, seam allowances and bindings in place on the reverse. With facings or bindings in place, work from the right side. Spread the seam open by holding either side of the presser foot and then stitching in the ditch created, catching the facing or binding in place on the reverse. The fabric will roll back slightly over the ditch and hide the stitches (diagram 3).

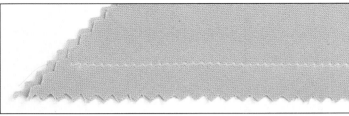

STRETCH STITCH

Stretch stitch – Used to stitch stretchy fabrics, this is a flexible stitch that is worked with two stitches forward and one back so that each stretch stitch is stitched three times. This creates a flexible seam that will stretch with the fabric. Many modern sewing machines have a choice of stretch stitches. Adjust the stitch length and width to suit the fabric (longer for heavy fabrics, smaller for lightweight fabrics).

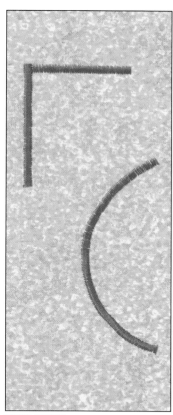

SATIN STITCH

Satin stitch – Used to cover raw edges and to attach appliqué, this is a very close zigzag stitch. Many modern machines have it as a utility stitch, but if not, set the machine for zigzag stitch and the stitch length to a minimum of 0.45. Reduce the stitch width to suit the fabric – narrow for smaller stitches and lightweight work and wider for heavier fabric or appliqué.

Helpful hint: Many of the zigzag-based stitches are difficult to unpick and can leave holes, so always test different stitches on a sample of the same fabric with the same number of layers and interfacings.

DIAGRAM 4

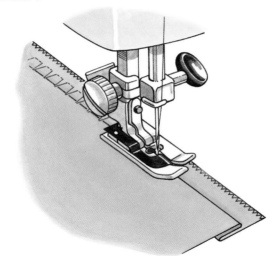

Blind hem stitch

This is a very neat hemming stitch which produces a softly rounded hem finish. When stitched by machine, a small ladder-like stitch is visible on the right side of the fabric. To minimize this, use matching thread. The stitch is formed by catching just a tiny amount in the garment and two or three stitches in the hem allowance. Neaten the raw edge before turning the hem allowance to the wrong side. Attach a blind hem foot, which has a metal guide and a shorter right toe, and place the fabric under the foot with the fold against the fabric guide. Ensure the needle just pierces the folded fabric close to the fold by adjusting the stitch width (diagram 4).

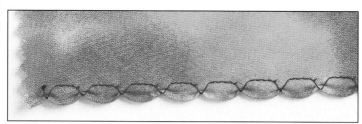

SHELL TUCK STITCH

Shell tuck stitch

Another hemming stitch, this is mainly used on bias-cut fabrics, knits or soft woven fabrics. Similar to blind hem stitch, it combines two or three straight stitches with a zigzag stitch. Sew along the fold so the needle on the right swing is clear of the fold to form the tucks.

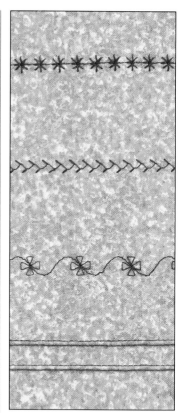

HEIRLOOM STITCHING

Heirloom stitching

This term encompasses many decorative stitches that are traditionally associated with heirloom projects such as christening gowns or table linen. Special needles are often used to help with the stitch effect, such as double or wing needles. Wing needles have a wider eye and are designed to leave holes as they stitch.

Corners and curves

Sooner or later you will come across projects that mean you have to sew curves or corners. There are some easy steps to take to handle them most effectively in order to produce a perfectly stitched, neat finish.

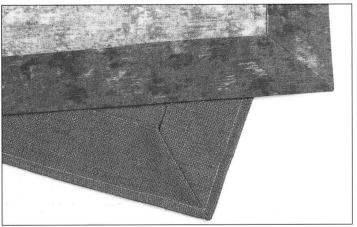

FABRIC CORNERS

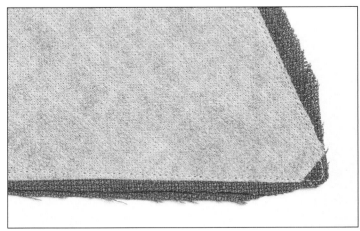

REDUCING BULK

Corners

Seams at corners often take extra pressure and need to be strengthened. Unless handled properly it can be difficult to achieve a neat crisp corner because of bulky fabrics.

Strengthening

Stitch with a regular stitch length to within 2.5 cm (1 in) of the corner, then reduce the stitch by 0.5–1 mm, depending on the fabric thickness, and stitch to the corner. Stop with the needle down, raise the presser foot, pivot the work slightly and then take 1–2 stitches diagonally across the corner. Raise the presser foot to pivot the work again, ready for the next seam. Stitch for 2.5 cm (1 in) before increasing the stitch length to a regular length again. Repeat for each corner (diagram 1).

DIAGRAM 1

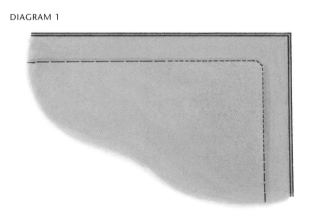

DIAGRAM 2

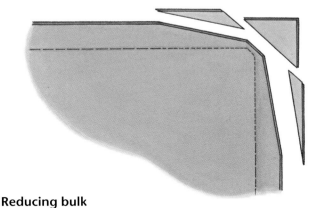

Reducing bulk

Trim the seam allowance diagonally across the corner. If the fabric frays easily, dab on some fabric glue or fray check and allow to dry before turning the corner out. For very sharp corners, cut the corner off diagonally and then cut wedges at the start of either seam to grade the bulk at the corner when turned through (diagram 2).

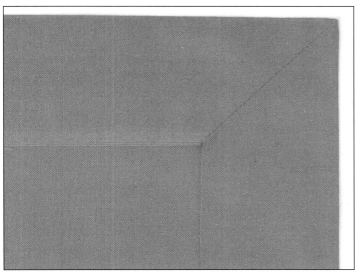

MITRED CORNER

Mitering

This is used to provide a neat angled corner for patch pockets, hem edges, borders and trims. Mitering corners also reduces bulk by cutting away some of the excess fabric. For a crisp mitred corner, follow these instructions:

- On either side of the corner, fold the seam allowances of both edges to the wrong side and press.
- Unfold and then refold the corner diagonally where the two creases cross, again to the wrong side. Press to make a crease (diagram 3).
- Unfold and then refold the fabric diagonally to bring the side edges together. Stitch across the diagonal. Trim the fabric close to the stitching and press the seam open.
- Turn the corner to the right side, using a point turner to push the corner out from the inside.

Curves

Fabric cut on the curve will have at least part of the edge cut on the grain, which means the fabric will be more stretchy. To prevent unwanted stretch at shoulders, neck edges or armholes, stay stitch (see Machine stitching, page 45) or add bias tape, a fusible curved tape that is fused within the seam allowance to prevent stretch.

To ensure curved areas lie flat when turned through to the right side, seam allowances need to be clipped or notched so they can overlap or spread. Outer (convex) curves are notched by taking small wedge shapes from the seam allowance at regular intervals, while inner curves only need small clips cut into the seam allowance (diagram 4).

NOTCHED OUTER CURVE

DIAGRAM 3

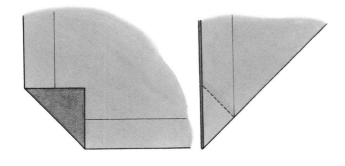

DIAGRAM 4

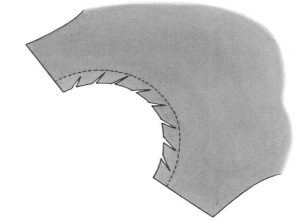

Seams

There are various seams that can be used to sew fabric layers together. Which to use depends on the fabric type and weight and the purpose of the seam.

General sewing tips

Whatever seam technique used there are a few steps to take to ensure perfect seaming every time:

- Before working on a project, try out the stitch technique on a fabric sample with the same number of layers and interfacings.
- Stitch all seams in the same direction, i.e. from top to bottom to prevent the fabric pulling and twisting in opposite directions.
- Once stitched, press the seams from both wrong and right side to embed the stitches. Always press before enclosing or crossing the seam with another row of stitching.

- Take care to maintain an even seam allowance (normally 1.5 cm (⅝ in) on garments and 6 mm (¼ in) on crafts). Seam allowances are provided to allow for adjustments and to prevent seams ripping apart during wear. Use the stitching guidelines on the throat plate (diagram 1). Most are marked in 3-mm (⅛-in) increments. Alternatively, use the edge of the presser foot or use masking tape to mark your own guide. On close-fitting garments or patchwork projects, mark the stitching line with a chalk pencil to ensure total accuracy.

DIAGRAM 1

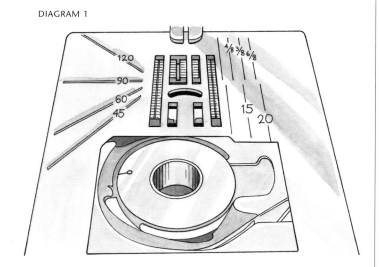

PLAIN SEAM

Plain seam

This is the most commonly used seam for woven fabrics, stitched with a straight stitch, usually 1.5 cm (⅝ in) from the raw edges. The stitch length depends on the fabric thickness and number of layers being seamed together. For lightweight fabrics use between 2–2.5 mm (10–12 spi), for medium-weight fabric 2.5–3 mm (8–10 spi) and for heavyweight fabrics between 3–4.5 mm (6–8 spi).

Helpful hint: *Avoid threads tangling at the start of a seam by holding both the bobbin and top thread tails behind the needle. Start approximately 2.5 cm (1 in) from the top of the fabric, stitch forward 13 mm (½ in) and then reverse to within 1.5 cm (⅝ in) of the top of the fabric before continuing forward again.*

Knit seams

Fabrics that stretch and need to remain flexible need seams that stretch also and thus should be stitched with a zigzag stitch of some sort. Use a regular zigzag stitch, three-step zigzag or a stretch stitch. All can have the length and width altered to make the stitching wider and further apart. For lightweight fabrics choose a smaller length and width and for heavier fabrics, a wider stitch length and width.

On some areas of knit fabrics – such as necklines and shoulders – it is necessary to prevent unwanted stretch. Stitch these areas with a straight stitch. For very stretchy fabrics add edge tape in the seam allowance (see Interfacings and stabilizers, page 28), which gives the fabric more stability, then stitch the seam with a straight stitch.

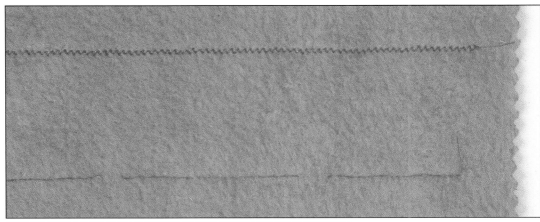
STRETCH FABRIC WITH ZIGZAG STITCHING AND BROKEN STRAIGHT STITCHING

KNIT FABRIC STABILIZED WITH EDGE TAPE

Double stitched seam

This is used to strengthen the seam in stretch fabrics or to stitch and neaten laces and sheer fabrics. In stretch fabrics, the extra row of stitching prevents the fabric curling. Stitch the first row along the seam line, using a straight stitch. Stitch the second row a scant 3 mm (⅛ in) away, stitching in the same direction, using either a straight or small zigzag stitch. Trim close to the outer stitching.

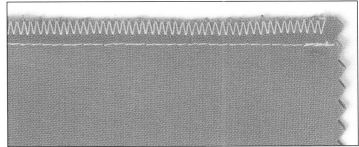
DOUBLE STITCHED SEAM

Bias seams

Again, bias-cut fabric has more stretch and thus has to be treated with care. To avoid rippling seams or unwanted stretch, stitch slowly, holding the fabric in front and behind the presser foot, slightly stretching it as you sew. Once carefully pressed, the stitching relaxes into a smooth seam. Heavier weight fabrics also need stabilizing to prevent them drooping and sagging.

To do this, add edge tape to the seam allowance.

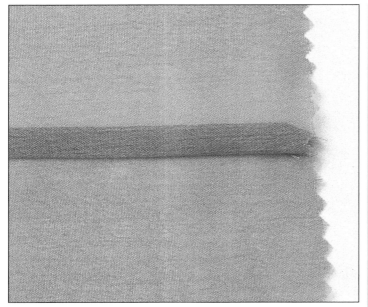

FRENCH SEAM

LAPPED SEAM

DIAGRAM 2

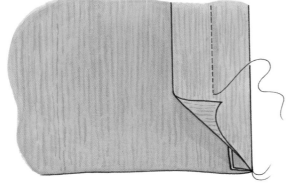

DIAGRAM 3

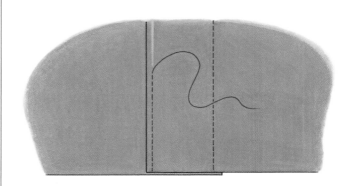

French seam

Ideal for sheers, lightweight fabrics, blinds and unlined curtains where the reverse is visible. French seams are created with two rows of straight stitching, first with the fabric wrong sides together, then with the fabric refolded right sides together. Stitch the first seam 1 cm (⅜ in) from the raw edges, trim to a scant 3 mm (⅛ in) and press. Turn the fabric so the right sides are together and the seam is on the fold, then stitch again in the same direction, 6 mm (¼ in) from the edge (diagram 2).

Lapped seam

This is perfect for fabrics that don't fray, such as faux suedes, leathers and fleece. The fabric is overlapped rather than sewn with right sides together. Again two rows of straight stitching are used. On the fabric that will overlap, mark the stitching line with chalk (see diagram), then trim the seam allowance away to within 2–3 mm (¹⁄₁₆–⅛ in) of this marked line. Place the cut edge over the other fabric piece, so that the marked stitching line just overlaps the stitching line of the under piece (note both pieces are right sides up). Stitch the first

row along the marked stitching line. Stitch again, in the same direction, 6–13 mm (¼–½ in) from the first row, catching the seam allowance of the under piece in the stitching (diagram 3).

Helpful hint: Lap vertical seams away from the centre and horizontal seams down. Avoid using pins on fabrics that mark – use double-sided basting tape instead.

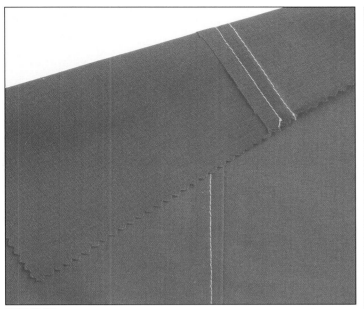

WELT SEAM

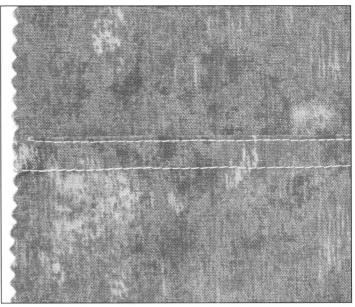

FLAT FELL SEAM

DIAGRAM 4

DIAGRAM 5

Welt and double welt seams

Similar to lapped seams, welt seams are particularly suitable for heavyweight fabrics. Again the seam is formed with two rows of straight stitching. The first is a regular seam with right sides together, the second is to catch the seam allowance. Having stitched the seam, grade the seam allowances, which reduces bulk, by trimming the under seam allowance to 6 mm (¼ in). Then, working from the right side, sew again 6–13 mm (¼–½ in) from the seam, catching the untrimmed seam allowance in the stitching. This will encase the trimmed seam allowance at the same time (diagram 4). A double welt seam has another row of stitching close to the seam line.

Flat fell seam

Used on sportswear and simple reversible garments, this seam technique sews and neatens the seam allowances, with the seam allowances on the right side of the fabric. As with French seams, stitch a regular seam with the wrong sides together then press the seam allowances together to one side. Trim the under seam allowance to 3 mm (⅛ in). Tuck under the raw edge of the upper seam allowance and press in place (if preferred baste in place), then stitch close to the fold from the right side.

Seam finishes

Unless seams are encased, they need to be finished, or neatened to prevent the fabric fraying during wear and to reduce bulk in the seam area. As with seaming, there are different methods to finish seams, depending on the type of fabric being stitched.

Reducing bulk

Although they do not need neatening, seam allowances that are encased may need to be reduced in order to reduce the bulk within the seam area. This can be done by clipping and notching (see Paper patterns, page 32), trimming and grading. Grading is simply cutting the two seam allowances to a different width which cuts down the bulk of the fabric and prevents unsightly ridges showing through on the right side. Trim the seam allowance closest to the main fabric to 6 mm (¼ in) and the under seam allowance to 3 mm (⅛ in) (diagram 1).

DIAGRAM 1

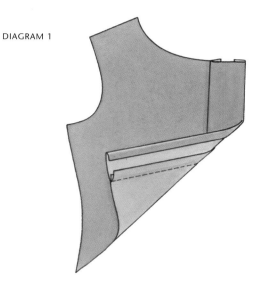

Pinked edges

The quickest way to neaten cottons and other lightweight fabrics is to cut the edges with pinking shears to within 6 mm (¼ in) of the seam. Press before and after cutting.

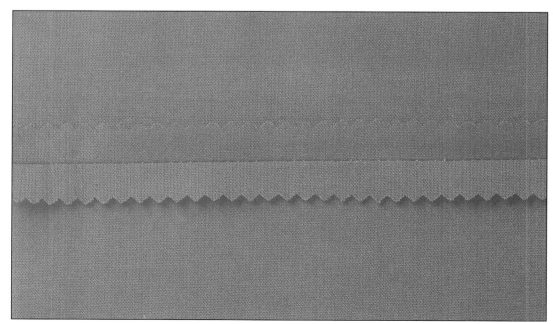

PINKED SEAM EDGE

Clean finishing

Press open the seam allowance then turn under the raw edges by 3 mm (⅛ in) and stitch in place with a straight stitch. This is suitable for light- to medium-weight fabrics.

Overcast or zigzag seam finish

This method involves using a zigzag stitch on woven fabric so the right swing of the stitch is just off the fabric edge. On knit fabrics, keep all the stitches on the seam allowance, then trim the seam allowance close to the stitching. Lightweight fabrics can have both seam allowances neatened together as one. On heavier weight fabrics, press the seam allowances open and neaten separately.

Bound seams

These are often used in tailored garments, particularly if the inside might be visible. Seam allowances are bound with bias binding tape or special tricot seam binding tape that folds in two, encasing the raw edges. Use a straight stitch on woven fabrics and a zigzag stitch on knit fabrics. Stitch through the tape and seam allowance, catching both the top and underside of the tape at the same time.

SEAMS BOUND WITH BIAS BINDING TAPE AND TRICOT SEAM BINDING TAPE

Top stitched seam

This is a seam finish that can be functional or decorative. It helps make the seam more durable as well as providing a crisp edge. For a decorative finish, use contrasting threads and any decorative stitch. For simple top stitching, use matching thread and a straight stitch. If sewing lightweight fabrics, press the neatened seam allowances together to one side, then, working from the right side, top stitch 6 mm (¼ in) from the edge, catching the seam allowance in the stitching. For heavier weight fabrics, press the seam allowances open and top stitch from the right side down both sides of the seam.

TOP STITCHED SEAM AND DOUBLE TOP STITCHED SEAM

Style techniques

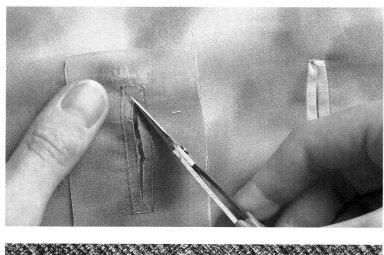

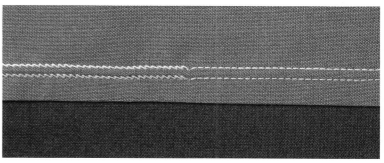

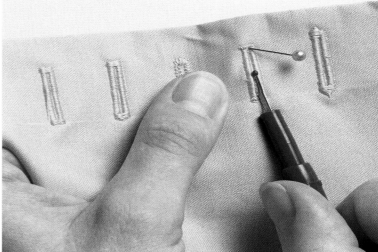

Hemming

There are a number of different ways to hem and different styles of hem. The main hemming techniques used in dressmaking are covered here.

General tips

1 Let a garment or curtains hang for 24 hours before hemming to allow the fabric to settle and drop. This is particularly important for garments cut on the bias or knit and loosely woven fabrics.

2 Apart from finishing off a garment or curtain, hems can help the drape by adding weight. Hem depths vary depending on the garment. As a guide, for straight dresses, skirts and coats, allow 5–7.5 cm (2–3 in). For trousers, flared and A-line hems allow 3–5 cm (1¼–2 in). Hems on curtains depend on fabric thickness and length of curtain and range from 5–15 cm (2–6 in).

3 Measure for length from the floor to desired length. Wear appropriate shoes to ensure the back and front are even.

4 To mark the hemline, place pins horizontally or mark with chalk.

5 Turn the hem allowance to the wrong side along the marked hem edge and pin at right angles close to the fold. Trim the hem allowance (see average hem depths above) (diagram 1). Working from the wrong side, turn the hem allowance up at the marked hemline, matching side seams. Insert pins at right angles close to the folded edge. If it is uneven, trim the

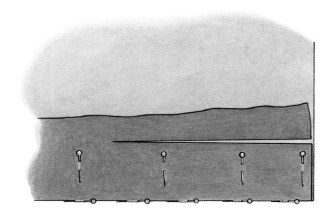

DIAGRAM 1

hem allowance to the depth required.

6 Always try garments on again when the hem is pinned in place before stitching, again wearing the appropriate shoes.

7 Garments which are A-line or have a curved hem will have extra fullness that needs to be eased in to prevent

ridges and folds at the hem. Ease stitch 6 mm (¼ in) from the raw hem edge and then gently pull up the bobbin thread to very slightly gather the excess. Spread it evenly and pin in place.

8 Choose a hem finish that is appropriate for the project – i.e. fluted lettuce hems on knit or very lightweight

transparent fabrics, bound hems on tailored suits, jackets and coats, blind hems on medium-weight fabrics and rolled hems on lightweight fabrics.

9 Having determined the correct hem allowance, neaten the raw edge on fabrics that ravel (fabrics that don't fray such as knits and fleece don't need neatening). On lightweight cottons, pink the edge with pinking sheers. On other fabrics, overcast or zigzag stitch or serge the edge. Turn up and finish by the preferred method (see page 59–61).

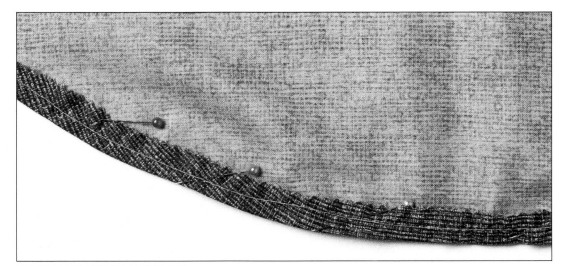

EASING IN FULLNESS ON CURVED HEM

Hem Finishes

Double hemming

Fold the hem allowance up, folding it again so the raw edge meets the first fold (diagram 2). Either top stitch or blind hem in place depending on the fabric weight and garment style. As the raw edge is encased, it is not necessary to neaten it.

DIAGRAM 2

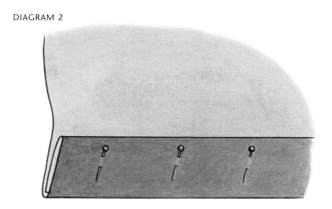

Top stitched hem

As with other top stitching, the stitches show on the right side. Suitable for lightweight fabrics and casual clothes, this is a quick hemming finish. Make a double hem as above (stretch knit fabrics and fleece can be folded once), then, working from the right side, stitch close to the inner fold. On heavier weight fabrics, fold up the hem allowance then tuck the raw edge under 1 cm (⅜ in), rather than make a double hem. Again top stitch close to the inner fold, working from the right side. Raw edges do not need neatening as they are enclosed within the stitching. To simulate a cover stitch hem (serger technique) stitch two parallel rows in the same direction or stitch with a widely spaced twin needle.

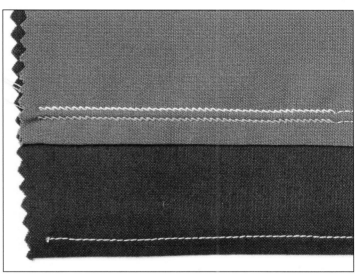

TOP STITCHED HEMS – TWIN AND NARROW STITCHING

Rolled hem

Ideal for lightweight and sheer fabrics, the hem allowance is minimal and thus doesn't look unsightly from the right side. If possible use a rolled hem presser foot through which the fabric is fed and rolled as it is stitched. If not, mark the hem length plus a hem allowance of just 3 mm (⅛ in). Fold up the hem and very lightly press. Stitch as close to the fold as possible, then trim away any excess hem allowance. Fold the hem again along the stitching, rolling the stitches just inside the hem and stitch again close to the inner fold.

ROLLED HEM

Lettuce hemming

Similar to rolled hems, lettuce or fluted hems look pretty on lightweight stretch fabrics. Prepare the hem allowance as for rolled hems, then using a small, close zigzag stitch, with the right swing of needle falling off the fabric, pull the fabric taut in front and behind the machine to stretch it as you sew. Alternatively use a serger with a slightly tightened needle tension, again stretching the fabric as you sew.

LETTUCE HEMMING

Blind hemming

Virtually invisible, blind hems are ideal for medium- and heavyweight fabrics, smart separates and suits. A machine stitched blind hem will leave a tiny ladder-like row of stitches on the right side. Use a thread to match the fabric to reduce visibility. Prepare the hem allowance as above, then fold the hem allowance to the wrong side before folding it back on itself so that 6 mm (¼ in) of the neatened hem edge is to the right of the fold. Use a blind hem foot, with the metal guard on the foot running alongside the fold. The blind hem stitch is a straight stitch (in the hem allowance) with a single left swing into the garment every few stitches (diagram 3). Once finished, fold the hem back out and press the stitching – do not press the hem edge as blind hems should have a rounded finish.

DIAGRAM 3

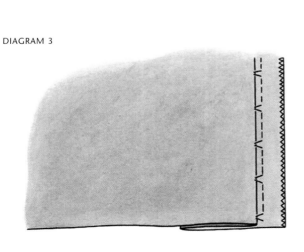

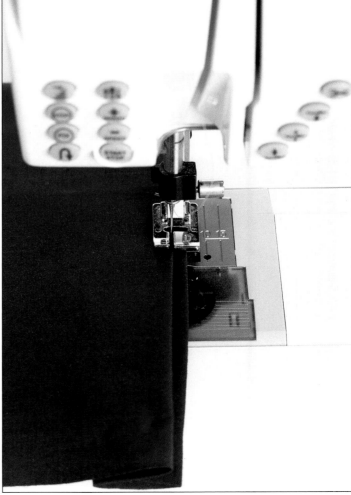

BLIND HEMMING ON A SEWING MACHINE

Taped hems

These provide a neat finish on garments where the hem might be seen, such as jackets and coats, or to extend the length of a garment. Use bias binding, ribbon or lace edging. To determine the amount of tape needed, measure the circumference of the garment and add 13 cm (5 in) for curves, corners and overlapping ends. Machine stitch the binding to the right side of the hem allowance 6 mm (¼ in) from the edge. Fold up the hem at the hemline and then hand stitch the tape in place with blind hem stitch (see Hand stitching, page 43).

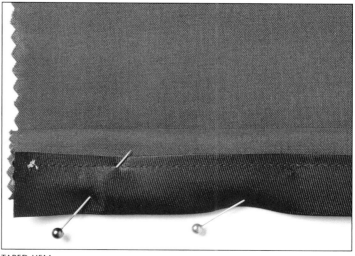

TAPED HEM

Leather or suede hems

To avoid stitching leather and suede use fusible hemming web. Reduce the hem allowance to a maximum of 1.5 cm (⅝ in) by trimming off the excess. Turn up the hem on the hemline and place the webbing between the fabric layers. Using a press cloth, press with a medium-hot dry iron. On heavyweight leathers, simply cut the hem at the hemline and leave unfinished.

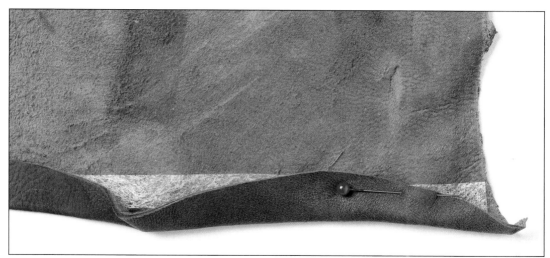

LEATHER HEM WITH WEBBING

Tailored hems

Tailored hems require a crisp finish, achieved by adding a strip of interfacing within the hem allowance. If sewing medium- or heavyweight fabrics, the drape and hang is helped with the addition of dress weights. These metal discs or lengths of chain are added to the hem allowance at the sides and front edges prior to final hemming.

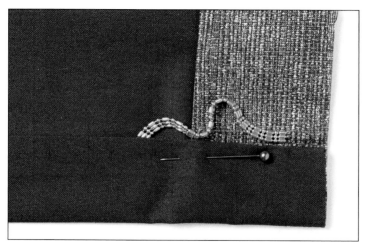

TAILORED HEM WITH INTERFACING AND DRESS WEIGHTS

Linings

Usually stitched with a top stitched double hem, lining hems should finish above the main garment or curtain hemline, ideally so the lining finishes at the top of the hem allowance on the main fabric.

Facings and bands

Facings and bands are used to neaten and finish garments at the neck, armhole, front and back openings. Usually cut from the same fabric as the garment, they are interfaced for added stability and then stitched, right sides together, to the garment edge before being turned to the inside.

Some jacket and coat designs have self-faced front openings, where the facing is cut as one with the jacket front and then folded back on itself to form the facing.

Helpful hint: When working with bulky, thick fabrics, cut facings from a lighter weight lining or cotton to reduce bulk at the neck, armhole or front.

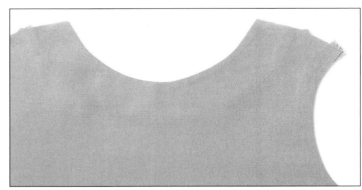

GARMENT FRONT WITH FACINGS AT NECK AND ARMHOLE

Handling tips

• Neck facings are generally curved, so they are cut across the grain and thus are prone to stretching. To prevent unwanted stretch, stay stitch the neck edge of the garment and the facing, stitching a normal stitch length just inside the seam allowance – 13 mm (½ in) from the raw edge (diagram 1).

DIAGRAM 1

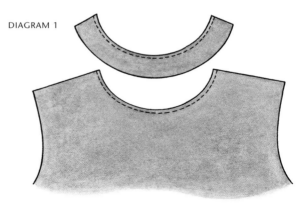

• Facings are interfaced over the whole piece whereas bands are interfaced along half the width. Trim fusible interfacing so that it fits just inside the seam line. After stitching the sew-in interfacing in place, trim close to the stitching to eliminate bulk from the seams.

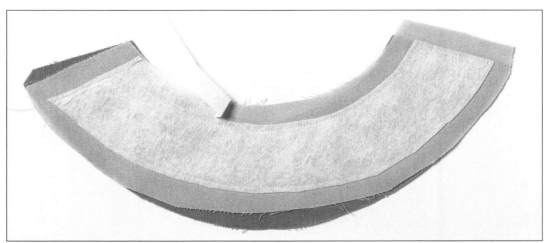

SEW-IN INTERFACING TRIMMED AFTER SEWING

• Bands are generally straight strips of fabric, cut along the straight of grain and folded in half lengthwise. Only half of the strip needs interfacing. As with facings, cut the fusible interfacing to sit just inside the seam line and butting against the fold line. Band width is a personal choice and depends on the garment style – kimonos, dressing gowns and coats suit a wider band, 10–15 cm (4–6 in) folded to 5–8 cm (2–3 in), whereas jackets suit narrow bands of 2.5–5 cm (1–2 in), folded to 6–25 mm (¼–1 in).

• Neaten the outer edge of the facing or band prior to sewing to the garment by turning the raw edge under and top stitching in place. Alternatively, use overcast stitch or serge the edge. Fabrics that don't ravel, such as fleece and stretch knits, do not need neatening.

• After stitching the facing or bands to the garment, right sides together, grade the seam allowances, trimming the garment edge to 6 mm (¼ in) and the facing to 3 mm (⅛ in). Clip and notch the curved areas, which will help the facing or band lay flat when turned through (diagram 2). Press with the seam allowance pressed toward the facing.

• To help prevent the facing from rolling out, under stitch the seam allowances to the facing only by opening out the facing and stitching close to edge, catching the seam allowances in the stitching (see Machine stitching, page 45). Turn the facing to the inside, rolling between thumb and fingers so the seam line falls just inside the edge. Press.

• To hem a band, stitch right sides together to the garment, fold the band in half lengthwise, again right sides together, and stitch across the ends from the fold to the raw edges (diagram 3). Trim the seam allowance and turn through. At the hem edge, stitch across the end the same depth as the hem allowance on the garment.

DIAGRAM 2

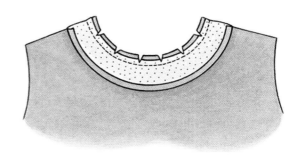

UNDERSTITCHING THE SEAM ALLOWANCES

DIAGRAM 3

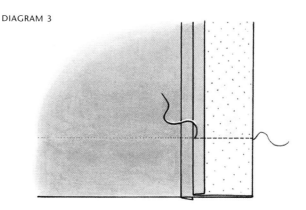

Darts

Darts help mould fabric to fit at the bust, waist and shoulders. They transform a flat piece of fabric into a figure-fitting garment.

A dart is usually wide at one end and tapered at the other (hence the name). When folded to the wrong side, it reduces the amount of fabric. Double-ended darts are used at the waistline to shape the waist, and are tapered to a point at either end, with the widest section in the middle. Generally stitched in a straight line from point to widest part,

darts are also occasionally stitched with a curved line for a closer fit.

Transfer any dart placement lines from the pattern to the wrong side of the fabric using chalk, pencil or tailor's tacks. If you are creating your own pattern, add darts for shaping at the bust and waist.

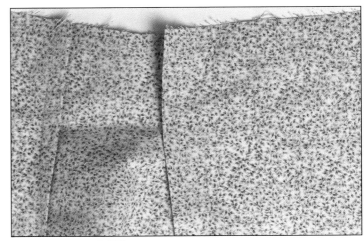

FABRIC PIECE WITH DARTS

Bust darts

Start just below the armhole at the side seam, tapering to a point 2.5 cm (1 in) from the fullest part of the bust. The top line of the dart is straight and the lower line angled up to complete the shaping. The dart size at the widest part is the difference between the bust at the fullest point and the chest measurement (taken under the arms, just above the bust). For very full busts, a further dart from the waist to the mid-bust point can also be added (diagram 1).

DIAGRAM 1

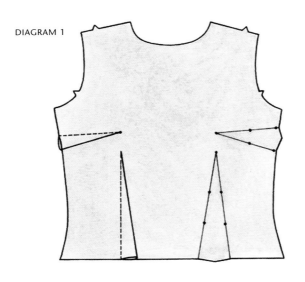

DIAGRAM 2

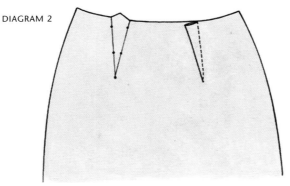

Waist darts

These are placed midway between the centre of the waist and the side seam, tapering to a point just above the hip (diagram 2). The amount of fabric to be folded into a dart at the widest point should not be more than 6.5 cm (2½ in), folding to 3 cm (1¼ in). To determine the dart size, divide the difference between the hip and the waist measurements by the number of darts being used (usually two at the front and two at the back). If the difference is 25 cm (10 in), the amount to be folded out will be 6.5 cm (2½ in) per dart.

Stitching darts

1 Fold the fabric right sides together at the dart placement, matching the widest dart positions and tapering the fold to nothing at the point. Pin in place.

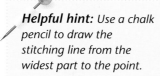

Helpful hint: Use a chalk pencil to draw the stitching line from the widest part to the point.

3 On heavyweight and thick fabrics such as fleece, cut the dart open along the fold, cutting as close to the point as possible. Press the dart seams open (diagram 3).

DIAGRAM 3

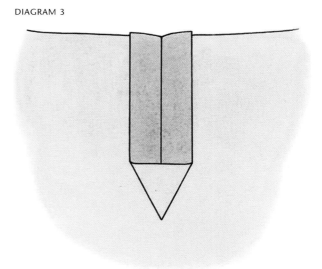

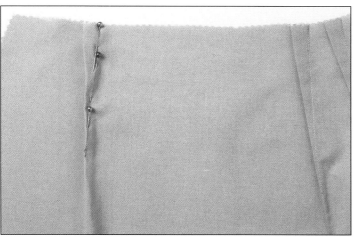

PINNING A DART IN PLACE

2 Stitch from the point on the fold towards the wide end of the dart. Secure the ends of the stitching with a lock or fix stitch or leave the thread tails and tie a knot at the end. Do not backstitch as this may cause a ridge in the fabric.

Press the stitching and then press the dart fold towards the centre if a vertical dart, and down towards the waist if a horizontal dart.

4 Fold the dart in the usual way and then machine stitch, starting at the centre, working towards the point at one end. Start at the centre again, overlapping a few stitches, then stitch to the other end. Again fix stitch or tie the ends rather than reverse stitch. Press to embed the stitches and then press the fold towards the centre.

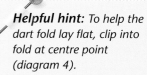

Helpful hint: To help the dart fold lay flat, clip into fold at centre point (diagram 4).

DIAGRAM 4

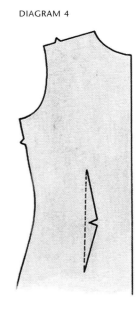

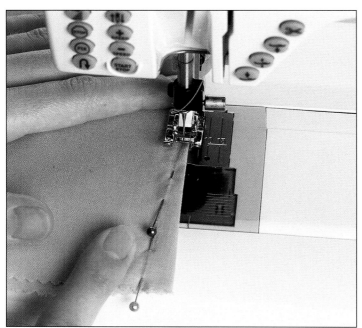

STITCHING FROM THE POINT ON THE FOLD

Pockets

There are three styles of pocket that can be added quite simply – patch pockets, in-seam pockets and hip line (jean style). If using commercial paper patterns, pockets are included in the pattern pieces and instructions.

Patch pockets

Formed from fashion fabric, these can be square, rectangular or have shaped ends. They are stitched on top of the garment. The easiest method is to self-line the pockets. Determine the pocket size and then cut the pocket shape double the length plus seam allowances of 1.5 cm (⅝ in) all round.

Fold the pocket in half, so the fold is at the top of the pocket, with the fabric right sides together. Stitch the sides and bottom, leaving a turning gap in the centre of the bottom edge (diagram 1).

Trim the seam allowances, cutting the corners at angles and turn through. Slip stitch the opening and then press. If desired, top stitch 6–13 mm (¼–½ in) from the top edge. Attach to the garment by edge stitching along the sides and bottom.

Helpful hint: Reinforce the top side edges by stitching in a small triangle (see below).

Lined patch pockets

If working with thick or bulky fabrics it may be preferable to line the pockets with lining fabric. Cut the pocket to size plus seam allowances of 1.5 cm (⅝ in) at the sides and bottom and 3 cm (1½ in) on the top edge in both the main and lining fabrics. Mark the fold line 3 cm (1½ in) from the top. Pin the lining to the main fabric, right sides together, along the top edge and stitch, taking a 6 mm (¼ in) seam allowance and leaving a turning gap in the centre.

At the marked fold line, fold the pocket top toward

the lining by 2.5 cm (1 in), pin and stitch the sides and bottom. Then trim the seam allowances and clip the corners at an angle before turning through the opening in the top (diagram 2). Slip stitch the opening and press. If desired, top stitch the pocket opening before positioning on the garment and edge stitching the sides and bottom.

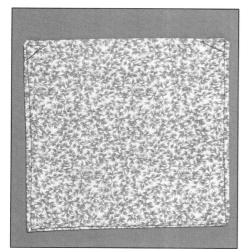

PATCH POCKET

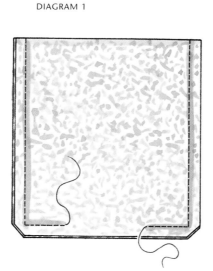

DIAGRAM 1

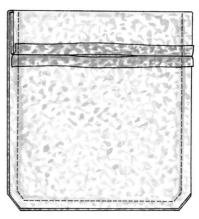

DIAGRAM 2

In-seam pockets

Generally found in the side seams of trousers, skirts and casual jackets, these pockets are attached to the front and back garment sections at the side edges and then the pocket bag is stitched at the same time as the side seam. They can be made from fashion fabric or lining, depending on the fabric weight.

The pocket shape is similar to a gloved hand, with a straight edge to attach to garment side approximately 8 cm (3 in) below the waist. With the right sides together, pin the straight edge of the pocket to the side seam and then machine stitch, taking the usual 1.5 cm (⅝ in) seam allowance. Neaten and press

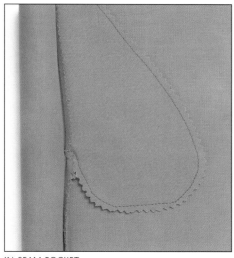

IN-SEAM POCKET

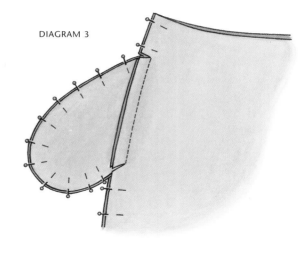

DIAGRAM 3

the seam allowance towards the pocket. Repeat with the other pocket section and trouser or skirt back.

With right sides together, pin the front to the back, with the pocket extending beyond the seam, pinning around the

pocket bag and down the side (diagram 3). Machine stitch, pivoting at the top and bottom of the pocket. Clip the seam allowance top and bottom of the pocket before pressing the pocket towards the front of the garment.

Hip line pockets

Also known as side slant pockets, these are shaped front pockets often found on jean-style trousers and skirts. They have two pocket parts, the facing and pocket back. The pocket facing can be cut from lining if the main fabric is thick or bulky.

Having cut the pocket sections, reinforce the opening edge of the pocket facing by stay stitching or adding edge tape or interfacing. Then with right sides together, stitch the facing to the garment front (diagram 4). Grade and clip the seam allowance. As extra reinforcement, press, then stitch the clipped seam allowance towards the pocket facing and under stitch (see Machine stitching, page 45). Turn the facing to the inside along the seam line and press.

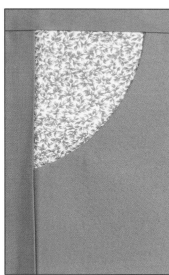

HIP LINE POCKET

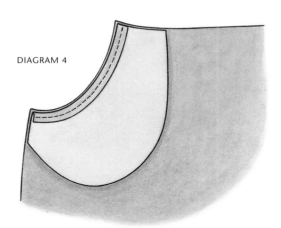

DIAGRAM 4

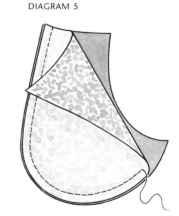

DIAGRAM 5

If desired, top or edge stitch close to the fold.

Again with right sides together, machine stitch the pocket facing to the pocket back around the outer edge (diagram 5). Neaten the raw edges with zigzag stitch. Then pin and stitch the garment side seam, catching the

straight edge of the pocket bag side in the seam. The top of the pocket bag will then be caught in the waistband seaming.

Waistbands

Waistbands add a reinforced stable section of fabric from which trousers or skirts hang and finish off the top of the garment.

Waistbands can have front, back or side openings. A comfortable fitting waistband is 13–25 mm (½–1 in) larger than the actual waist measurement. Alternative finishes at the waist include facings, and elasticated or drawstring waistbands (see Elastic and casings, page 96).

Waistband width – The width of the waistband depends on fashion, style and personal choice. An average is 4–5 cm (1½–2 in). Whatever the width required, the amount of fabric will be twice the width, plus seam allowances.

Waistband length – The length is determined by size, ease, overlap (if the waistband has an opening) and seam allowances. To the waist size add 2.5 cm (1 in) for comfort ease, 3 cm (1¼ in) for overlap, if required, and 3 cm (1¼ in) for the seam allowance for either end. Therefore for a size 12 (US size 10), 67 cm (26½ in) waist, you will need a length of waistbanding that is 75.5 cm (30 in).

Interfacing

Waistbands need to be interfaced to provide support and stability. There is a range of waistband interfacings available in different widths, some with perforations for easy folding and seaming, others with stiffeners to prevent waistbands creasing and rolling. For stretch fabrics and knits use a woven sew-in interfacing that has some give in it as well as support.

Always trim interfacing from within the seam allowance to avoid unwanted bulk (the waistband has three layers of fabric: front and back with neatened edge. A garment with pleats, darts and lining can add another 2–3 layers). Trim fusible interfacings to just within the seam allowance before fusing.

WAISTBAND ON GARMENT FRONT

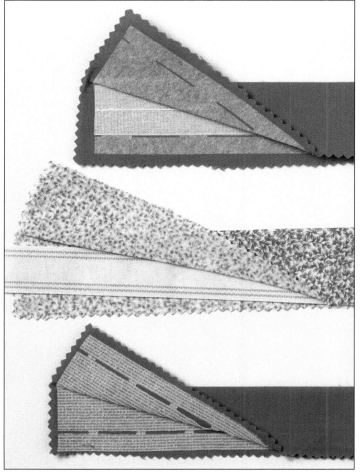

SELECTION OF WAISTBAND INTERFACINGS

Helpful hint: *To prevent fusible interfacings coming loose later on, allow to cool completely after fusing in place.*

Trim sew-in interfacings close to the stitching once they have been stitched in place. *Reducing bulk* – As well as trimming interfacing from seam allowances, bulk can be reduced by neatening the raw back edge of the waistband with serging (or use the fabric selvage which doesn't need neatening). An alternative is to interface just half the waistband width with a stiffener such as Petersham.

Sewing waistbands

1 Waistbands are attached to the garment after zipper insertion. Before attaching, neaten one long edge (the back edge) by overlocking or turning under by 6 mm (¼ in) and stitching in place.

2 Next pin the unfinished long edge to the garment, with one end overlapping the garment opening by 1.5 cm (⅝ in) and the other end overlapping by 3 cm (1¼ in) (diagram 1). Evenly distribute the remainder of the waistband along the garment top edge, matching notches and side seams if applicable. Stitch in place then trim and grade the seam allowances by trimming the garment seam allowance to 6 mm (¼ in) and the waistbanding allowance to 3 mm (⅛ in). Press the seam allowances toward the waistband.

3 Fold the waistband in half, right sides together to finish the ends. The neatened edge should just sit over the waistband seaming. Taking a 1.5 cm (⅝ in) seam allowance, stitch the overlap from the fold to the seam line. Pivot with the needle down and then stitch along the seam line to the start of the garment. At the other end, simply take a 1.5 cm (⅝ in) seam and stitch from the fold to the seam line. Trim the seam allowances close to the stitching, snipping the corners at angles and then turn the waistband through and press.

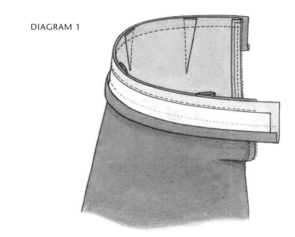

DIAGRAM 1

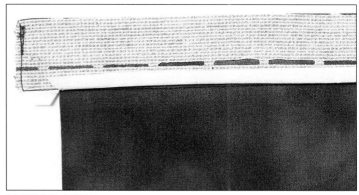

WAISTBAND OVERLAP

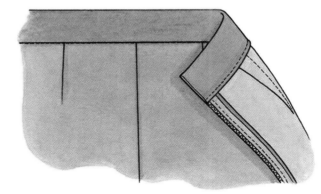

DIAGRAM 2

4 Slip stitch the neatened back edge of the waistband over the seam allowance on the inside or stitch in the ditch from the right side, pulling the garment and waistband apart as you stitch in the previous seam line and catching the underside of the waistband in place as you stitch (diagram 2).

5 Add a buttonhole to the overlap and buttons to the underneath layer (see Buttonholes, page 79) or hand sew a hook and eye fastener in place.

Collars

Collars consist of at least three layers, upper, interfacing and under collar. Sometimes there is also a facing. Different collar styles are used for different garments.

Collar types

Flat collar – Lies flat against the neck edge (diagram 1). Used on children's clothing, blouses, jackets and coats.

Rolled collar – Rises up from neck edge and then rolls down to the garment (diagram 2). The point at which the collar begins to fall is called the roll line. Used on shirts and jackets. Both flat and rolled collars have the upper and under collar cut on the straight of grain from the same pattern piece.

Standing collar – A simple band that rises up from the neck edge (diagram 3). It can be a single width band or a double width band that rolls back on itself. The stand can be straight or shaped. Used on casual tops, blouses and jackets. A shirt collar has an upright stand with a collar piece that folds down over the stand. The pieces may be separate or cut as one.

Sewing tips

- Select an interfacing that is slightly lighter in weight than the garment fabric and cut on the straight of grain to prevent the collar buckling. Attach interfacing to the upper collar section, trimming the interfacing to just within the seam line to reduce bulk in the seams.
- Make the under collar pattern piece 1–2 mm (¹⁄₁₆ in)

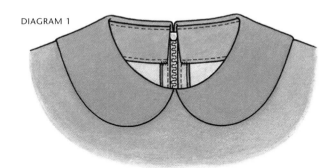

DIAGRAM 1

DIAGRAM 2

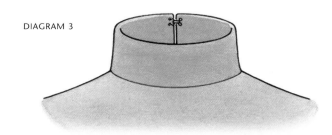

DIAGRAM 3

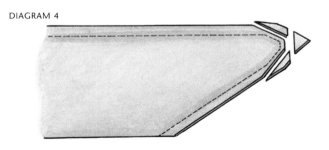

DIAGRAM 4

smaller than the upper collar section so the seam joining the two pieces rolls slightly to the underside.
- When sewing collar pieces, start in the centre and stitch towards either end.
- When stitching pointed collars, reduce the stitch length 2.5 cm (1 in) before and after the corner. Make one stitch diagonally across the corner and then cut triangular shapes from the seam allowances at the corner to reduce bulk (diagram 4).
- Always grade seam allowances – cutting the upper collar to 6 mm (¼ in) and the under collar to 3 mm (⅛ in). Clip and notch at the curves. Press from both sides before turning through. Use a point turner to ease out the collar point.
- Stay stitch the neck edge of the garment before attaching the collar. Pin the collar, right sides together at the centre back, shoulder seams and front, then clip into the seam allowance of the neck edge of the garment to fit the rest of the collar smoothly.

Sewing flat and rolled collars

Interface the collar as above. On rolled collars, interface the under collar as well as the upper collar. Add a further strip of interfacing to the roll line on the under collar section to provide additional support for the rise.

Pin and stitch the collar pieces, right sides together around the outer edge, leaving the neck edge open. Trim and neaten the seam allowances, clipping and

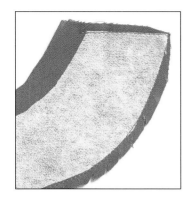

notching the curves. Press the seam allowance towards the under collar and then under stitch them in place to the under collar. Press again before turning right side out. Roll the seam between finger and thumb to set the seam slightly to the underside. Press in place.

If a flat collar is made up of left and right pieces, slightly overlap at the centre front and secure with basting stitches. Prepare the neck edge of the garment.

Without facing – Neaten the neck edge of the upper collar by turning under 6 mm (¼ in) and pressing. Next, pin the under collar only to the garment neck edge, keeping the upper collar free. Stitch in place then trim, clip and notch the seam allowance. Press towards the collar. Bring the neatened upper collar edge over the seam and slip stitch in place.

With facing – Pin and then stitch the complete collar to the neck edge with the under collar close to the garment. Press.

Add the facing, with the outer edge neatened, on top of the collar, right sides together. Stitch in place along the neck edge. Trim and grade the seam allowances, clip and notch curves. Note: the ends of the facing will overlap the garment edge at the back or front opening so they can be turned under and attached to the inside later (diagram 5).

Press the seams open and then press towards the facing. With facing opened out, under stitch the seam allowances to the facing close to the neck seam line. Turn the facing to the inside and press again. Attach to the garment at the shoulder seams and front or back opening, tucking the raw ends facing inside.

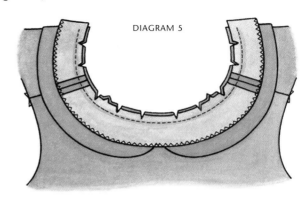

DIAGRAM 5

Stand collars

Having interfaced the collar section, fold in half and press to form a fold line. Unfold and tuck under one long edge by 6 mm (¼ in) and neaten. Refold the collar along the fold line, right sides together and stitch the short ends. Press the seams open, then towards the underside of the collar.

Turn the collar through to the right side, stitch the remaining long edge to the neck of the garment, keeping the neatened edge free. When working with woven fabrics, the garment neck edge needs to be notched and clipped to fit the stand collar. Slip stitch the neatened edge to the inside, encasing the seam allowances.

Stretch knit collars

Stretch fabrics are used for stand collars with no openings. Stitch a rectangular band into one piece by stitching short ends together.

Fold the band in half, right sides out, and mark into equal quarters. Turn the garment inside out and pin the collar

quarter marks to the centre front, centre back and shoulders, with the seam of the collar at the centre back. Sew in place with the collar uppermost, using a serger or an over edge stretch stitch, stretching the collar to fit the neck edge between the quarter marks. Remove the pins as you stitch (diagram 3).

SLIP STITCHING A STAND COLLAR TO THE NECK EDGE

DIAGRAM 6

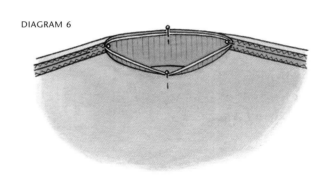

Sleeves

There are three main sleeve styles. The choice will usually be determined by the garment style. In addition to the style, sleeves can have a variety of hem finishes.

Sleeve styles

Set-in – These fit into a classic armhole. They can have a gathered or pleated sleeve cap. Puff sleeves are also set-in, with exaggerated gathering at the cap. They can be made of one or two pieces and may have elbow shaping created with small darts or ease stitching. Shirt sleeves, which have a smaller sleeve cap, can be attached to the garment back or front prior to the sleeve and side seams being stitched.

Raglan – These sleeves have a diagonal seam from the inner neck to the underarm. To

DIAGRAM 1

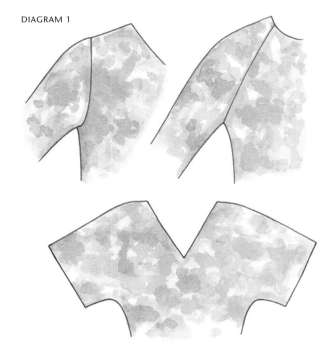

produce a closer fit at the top of the sleeve, a dart is inserted from the neck edge. A two-piece raglan sleeve will be joined to the front and back of the garment prior to the sleeve sections being joined.

Kimono – These sleeves are cut as one with the front and back of the garment. They can be capped or long, depending on style. Drop shoulder sleeves are a variation of the kimono style, where an additional rectangular sleeve is attached to the garment back or front before the underarm sleeve and side seams are sewn (diagram 1).

Sewing tips

- Sleeve patterns tend to have a double notch at the back and a single notch at the front which will match double or single notches on the back and front of the garment.
- Set-in sleeves may need ease stitching around the sleeve cap to help fit them into the armhole. Stitch two rows, with a slightly longer stitch length, just inside the seam allowance.

- Pin the sleeve in position, matching the top of the sleeve cap, notches and underarm seam. Pull up the ease stitching using the bobbin thread until the sleeve fits (diagram 2).
- Start stitching from the underarm seam with the sleeve uppermost.
- Trim the seam allowances and neaten with overcast or zigzag stitch.

DIAGRAM 2

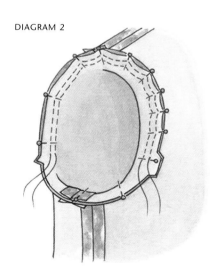

Hemming sleeves

Apart from cuffs and plackets (see Cuffs, page 74) sleeves can be finished with a simple double hem, with self-casing and a ruffle or bias binding (ideal for sheer fabrics where the inside of the hem is visible).

Self hem – On light or medium-weight fabrics, turn a double hem by turning under 1 cm (⅜ in) twice, with the raw edge touching the first fold. Top stitch in place, working from the right side. On heavyweight fabrics, neaten the hem edge with zigzag or overlock stitch and then turn up the hem allowance. Either top stitch from the right side or slip stitch the inside to the garment by hand.

Gathered with self-casing – This is formed by folding the hem allowance to the inside and stitching along both edges (raw and fold) to form a casing. Leave a gap in the upper row of stitching into which the elastic can be inserted. Insert the elastic and sew the ends together securely before closing the gap with slip stitching. Alternatively, gather the end of the sleeve with a long gathering stitch and attach a separate cuff as detailed on pages 74–75 (diagram 3).

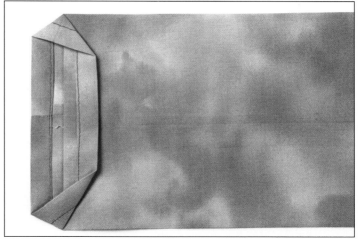

DOUBLE HEMMED SLEEVE WITH TOP STITCHING

Helpful hint: On thick, bulky fabrics, trim the seam allowance of the underarm seam within the hem allowance area to reduce bulk prior to turning up the hem.

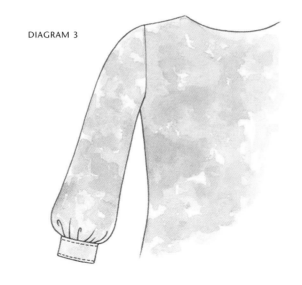

DIAGRAM 3

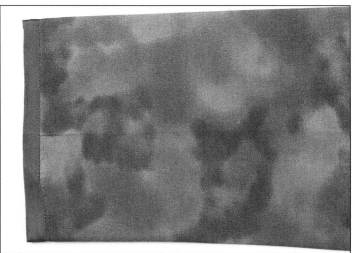

BIAS BOUND SLEEVE

Ruffle – A ruffle adds extra length to the sleeve in order to create a self-faced casing. The amount to add depends on the required depth of the ruffle – allow 13–15 cm (5–6 in) for a 8–10 cm (3–4 in) ruffle, plus casing. Neaten the raw edge of the sleeve, turn up at the hem length and then stitch close to the neatened edge and then again approximately 2.5 cm (1 in) away from the first row to form a casing. Leave a gap in the first row into which the elastic can be inserted.

Bias Binding – Open out the bias binding along one long edge and then pin to the sleeve edge, right sides together. Turn the raw end closest to the garment over to neaten the raw edge. Overlap the ends and machine stitch along the preformed foldline of the bias binding (diagram 4). Trim the seam allowances and turn the binding to the inside, encasing the raw edges. Stitch in the ditch from the right side, catching the bias trim in place or slip stitch in place by hand.

DIAGRAM 4

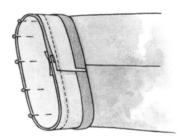

Cuffs

Cuffs can be simple bands, have plackets, a continuous lap, a hemmed opening or can be cut from contrasting fabric such as fur or knit rib.

Simple cuffs

Sleeve cuffs are generally formed from a top layer, interfacing and under layer or facing. The top and facing are often cut as one piece and folded in half, with the top half interfaced. Cuffs, also known as turn-ups on trousers or short sleeves, are made from an extended hem edge that is shaped to turn up easily.

This method creates a cuff from one piece of fabric, folded to form cuff and facing.

1 Cut a rectangle that is wrist circumference, plus 8 cm (3 in) for wearing ease and seam allowances, by approximately 16 cm (6¼ in) wide. Interface half the width, excluding the seam allowance and then neaten the other long edge (diagram 1).

2 With right sides together, fold the cuff in two lengthways, so the neatened edge overlaps the raw edge by 1.5 cm (⅝ in). Stitch the side seams, taking a 1.5 cm (⅝ in) seam allowance. Trim, cutting the corners at angles and turn through, using a point turner to push the corners out neatly.

Hemmed opening cuffs

Before adding the cuff, make a small hem opening at the sleeve hem by reinforcing the stitching 3 cm (1½ in) either side of the underarm seam, stitching along the seam line. Clip up from the hem edge to the stitching at either end, taking care not to cut the stitching, then turn the flap up and the raw edge under again. Stitch in place (diagram 2).

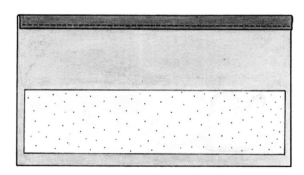

SIMPLE CUFF BAND ATTACHED TO SLEEVE

DIAGRAM 1

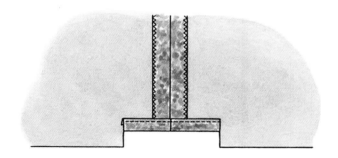

CUFF WITH HEMMED OPENING

DIAGRAM 2

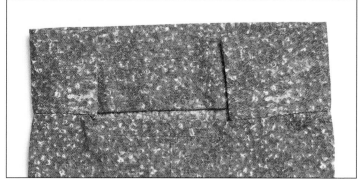

Seam opening cuff

An alternative to the continuous lap cuff, this is a simple method of creating a wider cuff opening. Stitch the sleeve seam to within 8 cm (3 in) of the end and press the seam allowance open. Neaten the raw edges to the end of the seam stitching. Snip into the seam allowance at right angles and then turn the remaining seam allowance under to hem. Machine stitch in place down both sides of the opening and across the top (diagram 3).

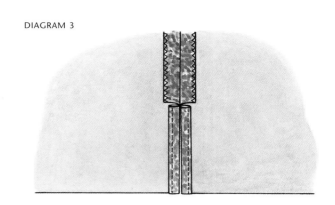
DIAGRAM 3

Continuous lap cuff

This is created in the sleeve fabric, approximately 10–13 cm (4–5 in) from the sleeve seam and is applied prior to stitching the seam. It is the most widely used opening, although it is not recommended on bulky fabrics.

1 Cut a bias strip of self fabric 3 cm (1½ in) wide and 15 cm (6 in) long. Turn one long edge to the wrong side and press.

2 Mark an upturned V shape, 8 cm (3 in) long and 3 cm (1½ in) wide at the sleeve edge. Stitch the V, reducing the stitch length just before and after the point then cut up the centre of the V almost to the stitching at the point. Spread open the slashed edge and then pin, right sides together, the raw edge of the bias binding to the slash.

Machine stitch in place. Turn the neatened binding edge to the inside, encasing the raw edges and slip stitch in place (diagram 4).

3 Refold the lapped edges to bring the hem edge back in line, with the front part of the lap to the inside. Stitch the underarm seam.

CONTINUOUS LAP CUFF

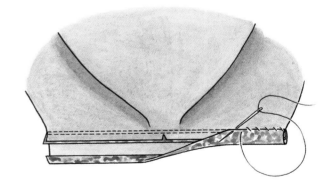
DIAGRAM 4

Attaching cuffs

Pin then stitch the raw edge of the prepared cuff to the sleeve edge, right sides together, matching the openings. Trim and grade the seam allowances and press towards the cuff. Fold the facing to the inside, covering the seam allowances and slip stitch in place.

Alternative cuff finishes also include vents (for tailored jackets) and plackets (used for men's shirts). Plackets are made from separate fabric pieces that are contrasting or of the same fabric and are attached to the sleeve opening (diagram 5).

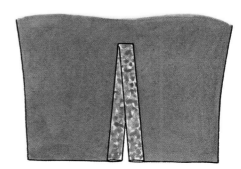
DIAGRAM 5

Zippers

Zippers can be inserted in two main ways – centred or lapped. In addition there are different types of zipper: some are used as decorative detailing, while concealed zippers are hidden within the seams of a garment to be virtually invisible.

SELECTION OF ZIPPERS

Zipper types

Nowadays these come not only with nylon or metal teeth, but also with decorative teeth such as clear, crystal, silver and coated. Lightweight zippers have nylon zipper tapes and teeth. Heavier metal zippers have cotton tapes. Zippers also come in a number of lengths and colours to suit most applications – including continuous (you cut to the length required) and double-ended.

Centred zippers – These are stitched with equal edges that meet in the centre of the zipper teeth. The stitching shows from the right-hand side of the garment. Used for dresses, front closure on jackets etc. and on soft furnishings

Lapped zippers – These are stitched so that one side of the zipper is attached to the edge of the folded-under seam allowance, the other to the seam line so that when it is closed, the fabric laps over. Only one side of the stitching shows from the outside. Used on trousers and skirts. A fly front zipper is similar, with a wider lap.

Helpful hint: *If the correct zipper length is not available, buy a zipper longer than required and hand stitch a bar tack across the bottom to the length required (stitch 5–6 times on the same spot across the teeth) to prevent the zipper tab coming off. Cut away the excess zipper (diagram 1).*

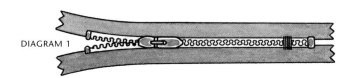

DIAGRAM 1

General sewing tips

- Neaten the seam allowance of seams that will have a zipper prior to zipper insertion.
- Position the zipper so that there is room for facings, waistbands, collars etc.
- If adding a zipper to lightweight or stretchy fabrics, add edge tape or lightweight interfacing to the seam allowance of the area in which zipper is to be inserted to improve stability.
- Use a special zipper foot on the sewing machine to allow stitching close to the teeth (concealed zippers need a special concealed zipper foot).

Centred zipper

1 Pin the seam, right sides together, and position the closed zipper in place. Mark the base of the zipper. Remove and baste the seam from the top to the mark, then change to a regular stitch length to finish the seam from the mark to the hem (diagram 2). Press the seam allowance open.

2 Replace the zipper, right side down, with the teeth in the centre of the basted seam line. Baste the zipper tape in place on both sides, basting through the seam allowance and the main fabric.

CENTRED ZIPPER IN PLACE

DIAGRAM 2

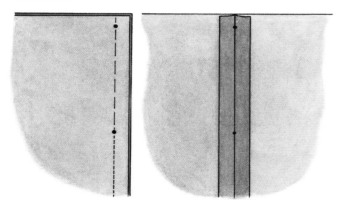

3 Working from the right side and using a zipper foot, machine stitch from the bottom of the zipper at the seam, stitch a few stitches then pivot and stitch up the side to the top. Repeat for the other side, again starting at the centre bottom of the zipper. Remove the basting.

Helpful hint: As you get close to the zipper pull, stop stitching, with the needle down and the foot raised. Open the zipper, working the pull past the presser foot. Finish stitching the side.

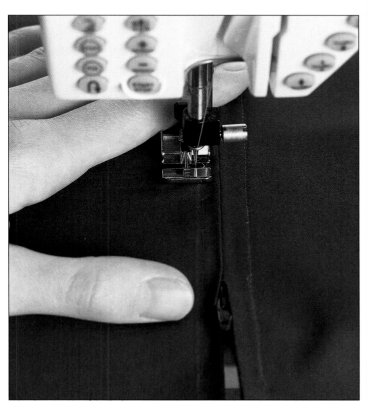

STITCHING SECOND SIDE OF CENTRED ZIPPER FROM RIGHT SIDE OF FABRIC

Lapped zipper

1 Mark the zipper position, baste and stitch the seam as for the centred zipper.

2 Unzip the zipper and with right side down, place on the left seam allowance so the teeth are on the seam line. Pin and baste to the seam allowance only, basting down the centre of the zipper tape (diagram 3).

3 Close the zipper, then turn it face up, creating a fold in the seam allowance along the teeth edge. Machine stitch as close to the teeth as possible with a zipper foot, starting at the zipper bottom (diagram 4). Clip the seam allowance below the zipper end.

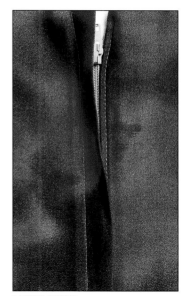

LAPPED ZIPPER

DIAGRAM 3

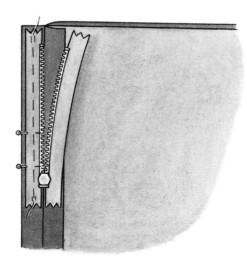

DIAGRAM 4

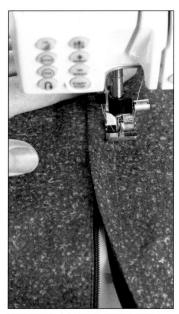

STITCHING A LAPPED ZIPPER FROM THE RIGHT SIDE OF THE GARMENT

4 Working from the right side of the garment, smooth flat, checking the zipper is even and flat also. Baste the right-hand zipper tape through all thicknesses across the bottom and up the side, approximately 13 mm (½ in) from the seam line. Machine stitch along the basting stitching, again working from bottom to top.

Open ended/ separating zipper

Zippers that open at both ends can be inserted using the centred or lapped zipper methods. They are often made from heavier weight fabric and metal teeth and are used on sportswear, vests and jackets. Insert zippers before adding front facings and hemming. For easy and quick insertion, separate the zipper and work with each half separately before rejoining.

Concealed zippers

The concealed zipper is a special type of zipper that has no coils showing on the right side of the zipper tape and thus is virtually invisible from the right side of garment. This zipper is inserted into a seam prior to the seam being constructed. In order to be properly stitched in place, you need to use a concealed zipper presser foot.

1 Open the zipper and press the coils of the zipper open with an iron to keep them away from the zipper tape.
2 On the left-hand garment section, place the right side of the zipper onto the right side of the fabric. Position the zipper so that the coils align with the stitching line 1.5 cm (⅝ in) from the cut edge. Baste in place (diagram 5).
3 Keeping the zipper open and using a concealed zipper foot, machine stitch the zipper in place so that the coils feed through the left-hand groove in the foot. Stop when the machine foot touches the puller on the zipper and fix the machine stitch.
4 Close the zipper. Position the right-hand side of the garment over the left-hand side of the garment, aligning the cut edges. Pin the zipper in position on the right-hand garment section. Open the zipper again and baste in place.
5 Machine stitch in place, this time with the coils feeding through the right-hand groove in the machine foot.
6 To complete the seam below the zipper, close the zipper and pin the remainder of the seam together. Using a regular zipper foot, stitch the seam, starting as close to the end of the zipper as possible (pull the end of the zipper tape away from the seam at the start). Press the seam allowance open.
7 Secure the last 5 cm (2 in) of the zipper tape to the seam allowance.

CONCEALED ZIPPER

DIAGRAM 5

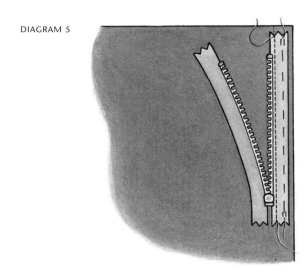

Buttonholes

When the correct combination of fabric, stabilizer or interfacing, thread and sharp needle are used, beautiful buttonholes are easily achieved on today's modern sewing machines, whether in one, three or more steps.

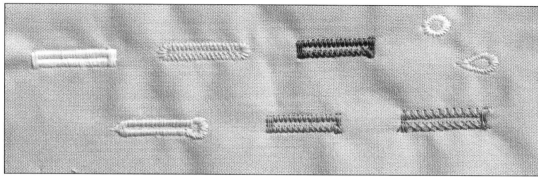

SELECTION OF BUTTONHOLES

Basic buttonholes

A basic buttonhole comprises a bar tack at either end and two sides which are closely satin stitched. Depending on your sewing machine, this might be stitched in one operation (one step) or require dials or buttons to be turned after each step – first side, bar tack, second side, final bar tack. Check your user's manual to determine the buttonhole functions you have.

General sewing tips
- Interface or stabilize the buttonhole area with fusible interfacing or tearaway stabilizer (see right).
- Use a general-purpose thread in both the bobbin and as the top thread.
- As the buttonhole comprises dense close stitching, penetrating at least three or more layers, use a new sharp needle so that it can pierce three or more layers of fabric easily.

- Determine the buttonhole size by measuring the button circumference. Halve the measurement and add 3 mm (⅛ in). Unusually shaped or domed buttons may require larger buttonholes.
- Always test buttonholes on fabric scraps, with the same fabric layers and interfacing prior to stitching on the garment.
- Once stitched, feed the thread tails back through the stitching before cutting them off.

Helpful hint: *Special-purpose buttonhole thread can be used for heavyweight garments which require very strong buttonholes.*

Stabilizing the buttonhole area

Buttonholes can be successfully stitched in any fabric, from lightweight sheers to heavyweight or stretch knits. To achieve a neat buttonhole, the fabric needs to be stabilized with interfacing or stabilizer to prevent the concentrated stitching puckering the fabric if it is lightweight, or stretching if it is a knit fabric. Most areas that require buttonholes are usually already interfaced – facings, waistbands, front openings etc. However, if they are not, add a small square of tearaway stabilizer behind the area to be stitched to provide the stability needed. It will also help the buttonhole retain shape when in use. If stitching very lightweight chiffons, add a further layer of water-soluble or tearaway stabilizer to help prevent the fine fabric being pulled down into the feed dogs (see Interfacings and stabilizers, page 28).

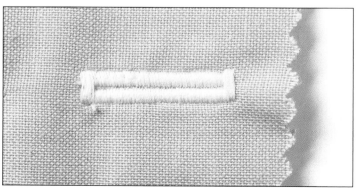

BASIC BUTTONHOLE

Marking the buttonhole positions

Buttonholes should be positioned at least 2 cm (¾ in) from the garment edge. On average, buttons should be placed approximately 5–8 cm (2–3 in) apart on garments and 10–13 cm (4–5 in) apart on soft furnishings. On lightweight fabrics, position them slightly closer.

Mark the buttonhole placement with chalk lines or basting stitches. For horizontal buttons, draw two parallel lines the buttonhole size apart, down the length to be buttoned. Draw the buttonhole positions in. For vertical buttons, draw a vertical line from top to bottom of the buttonhole placement and then mark the buttonhole size with tiny horizontal lines, spacing them evenly down the placement line. Note: Commercial patterns will have buttonhole placement marks on the tissue; transfer these marks to the fabric (diagram 1).

DIAGRAM 1

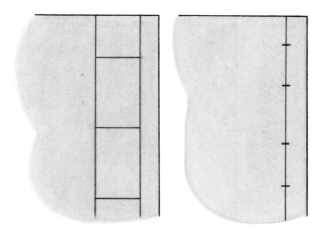

Opening the buttonhole

To open a buttonhole, place a pin at one end close to the inner edge of the bar tack and, starting from other end, push a seam ripper (quick unpick) towards the pin and between the side stitching.

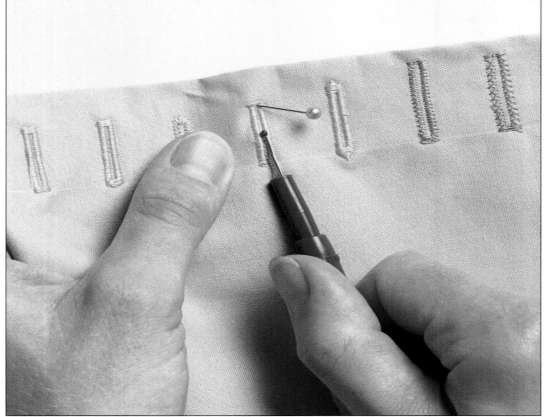

OPENING A BUTTONHOLE

Bound buttonholes

These designer-style buttonholes have lips either side of the opening. They are quite awkward to do, so are best avoided on fabrics that fray easily.

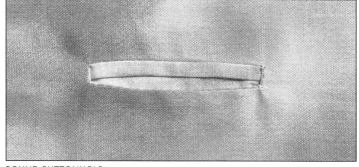

BOUND BUTTONHOLE

1 Cut a rectangle of fabric 5 cm (2 in) longer than the buttonhole and baste to the right side of the garment, centred over the buttonhole position. (To help centre accurately, fold a rectangle in half and crease the fold. Open out and place the crease over the buttonhole.)

2 Mark the buttonhole position plus a rectangle around the buttonhole, 3 mm (⅛ in) away from the marked line on either side.

3 Machine stitch the rectangle, counting the number of stitches taken on the short ends to ensure both are the same (diagram 2).

4 Starting at the centre and using a small pair of sharp scissors, cut the buttonhole down the length and then diagonally toward the corners of the rectangle, taking care not to cut the stitching.

5 Push the patch through the buttonhole, rolling the seam so it is on the edge of the buttonhole. Press.

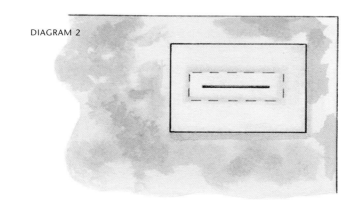

DIAGRAM 2

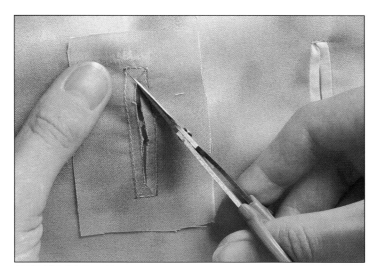

CUTTING INTO THE CORNERS OF THE BUTTONHOLE

DIAGRAM 3

6 Form the buttonhole lips by folding the long edges over the opening with the folded edges meeting at the centre of the buttonhole. Check the lips are even from the right side and then baste to hold in place.

7 Working from the right side of the garment, fold the garment back along the side of the buttonhole, exposing the ends of the patch. Stitch across, through all layers of the patch, close to the garment fold. Repeat at the other end of buttonhole (diagram 3).

8 Do the same at the top and bottom of the buttonhole – fold the garment back to expose the patch and stitch inside the original stitching line. Open out the garment and press with a press cloth.

Fastenings

These include buttons, button loops, hooks and eyes, hook and loop and snap fasteners. Zippers and buttonholes are covered in separate chapters.

SELECTION OF BUTTONS

SELF-COVERED BUTTONS

Buttons

Buttons come in many shapes and sizes but with just two types of sewing attachment – sew-through holes or a shank. Shanked buttons are best used on thicker fabrics and multi-layers. Sew-through buttons are ideal for lightweight garments.

General sewing tips

- Position buttons 3 mm (⅛ in) in from the outer edge of the horizontal buttonhole and 3 mm (⅛ in) from the top of the vertical buttonhole.
- Stitch with a double strand of general-purpose thread.
- When attaching sew-through buttons, place a small stick (match or cocktail) over the button and take stitches over the stick, taking 3–4 stitches through each hole. Remove the stick and pull the button up so the excess thread is between the button base and the fabric. With the needle between the button and the fabric, wind the thread around the stitching to form a small thread shank (diagram 1). Take the needle to the reverse of the fabric and tie off.

DIAGRAM 1

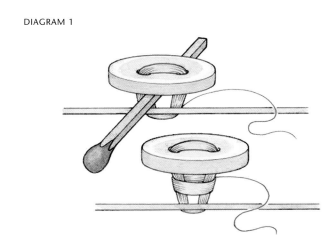

Self-covered buttons

Ideal when a perfect match is desired, or when suitable buttons are unavailable, self-covered buttons come in various sizes and in plastic and metal. Instructions to cover are included in packaging.

- If you are using lightweight fabric, cover metal buttons with lightweight interfacing or use a double layer of fabric.
- Avoid bulky fabrics or loosely woven fabrics which will be hard to gather and clip in the button back. Instead cover with similarly coloured medium-weight fabric.

Button loops

Used instead of buttonholes, button loops are often a decorative detail on jackets and bridal dresses and are combined with round or unusual-shaped buttons which might be difficult to slip through buttonholes. Loops can be made from strips of bias-cut fabric, from braid or purchased as ready-made loops on a tape.

Looped tape – Sandwich the tape between the main fabric and the facing, with the tape edge matching the garment edge and the loops to the inside. Stitch through all thicknesses close to the loops (diagram 2). When turned through the loops will stand proud of the fabric edge.

Self-fabric button loops – Cut a bias strip approximately 2 cm (¾ in) wide by the length needed. Cut a length of string 13 cm (5 in) longer than fabric (this is used to help turn the bias strip through to the right side). Fold the fabric in half, right sides together, with the string inside the fold. Stitch across one end, catching the string

end in the stitching and taking a 1 cm (⅜ in) seam. Without trimming the seam allowances (which will help fill out the tube), pull free the string end to pull the fabric through. Cut off the string.

Measure the buttons and then cut the fabric tube into suitable lengths, remembering to allow 1.5 cm (⅝ in) at either end for seam allowances. Pin the loops in position to the right side of the garment edge, with loops facing in and raw edges matching. Hand baste in position before adding facing as for the looped tape.

DIAGRAM 2

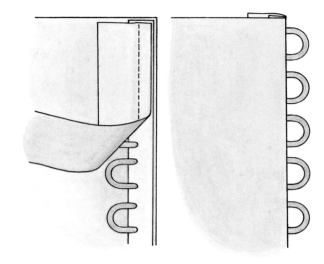

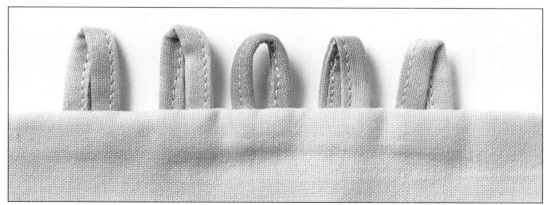

SELF-FABRIC BUTTON LOOPS

Hooks and eyes

Ranging in size and weight, these two-piece fasteners have a hook on one piece and an eye (loop) on the other. They can be used as an additional fastener at the top of zippers or alone. Use double thread or buttonhole twist thread to sew in place.

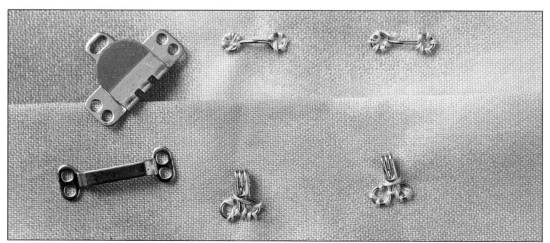

SELECTION OF HOOKS AND EYES

Snaps

Snaps, or poppers, are another fastener used on areas that will not take much strain. Ideal for children's clothing, they are easily pushed or 'snapped' together to fasten. Like hooks and eyes, they come in two parts, a ball and a socket. Place the ball section on the under lap of the garment and the socket on the overlap. Stitch with double thread.

SNAPS OR POPPERS AND SNAP TAPE

In additional to individual snap fasteners, snap tape is available on which the snaps are evenly spaced. These are ideal for bed linen and babies clothing. Separate the tape sections and stitch one side to one fabric edge, stitching along both long edges of the tape. Stitch the corresponding tape in position on the matching fabric, ensuring the snaps are lined up.

Helpful hint: Prevent the stitching showing on the right side of the garment by just picking up one or two fibres from the inside of the main fabric when stitching the socket in place. Stitch two to three times through each hole on the socket.

Hook and loop fastener (Velcro)

Again, a two-part fastener, this is made up of two strips of nylon, one with tiny hooks and the other with a fluffy looped side. When placed together the hooks grab the loops and hold firm. Available in different widths and colours, some hook and loop fasteners are fusible, others are sew-in or have one strip to sew-in and the other fusible – useful when attaching curtains to wooden battens etc. Also now available are single strip hook and loop tapes, which have both hooks and loops on the same strip.

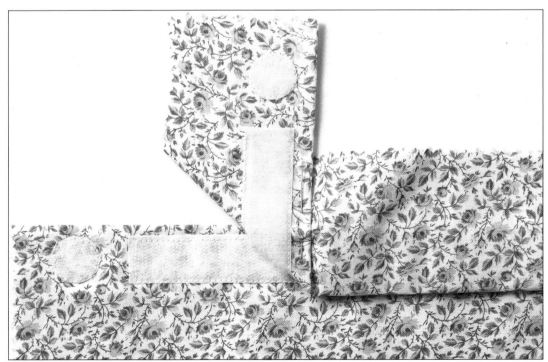

HOOK AND LOOP FASTENER ATTACHED TO FABRIC

Tucks and pleats

Tucks and pleats are formed by folding fabric back on itself to take in excess fabric, provide shaping or simply to create a design detail. Because they are created by fabric folds, more fabric is required than normal. How much extra is required will depend on the number and size of the pleats. Tucks are generally smaller than pleats and are sewn in place along the folded edge whilst pleats tend to be sewn at the top, or part of the way down only.

Tucks

Not only do tucks add decorative detail, they can also be used to help with fit. It is important to measure and sew tucks accurately to ensure the correct amount of fabric is tucked – a difference of just 3 mm (⅛ in) per tuck could affect the fit. For example, eight tucks, each out by 3 mm (⅛ in), equals an overall difference of 2.5 cm (1 in).

Tucks are taken along the straight grain, parallel with the selvages or fabric threads. Press vertical tucks away from the centre front or back and horizontal tucks downward.

There are three main types of tuck: pin, corded or wide.
Pin tuck – Often used on blouses, pin tucks are very narrow. Used on fine lightweight fabrics.
Corded – Formed by laying a cord within the fold of the fabric, resulting in a small raised tuck.

Wide tuck – A wider version of a pin tuck and similar to a pleat.

SELECTION OF TUCKS AND PLEATS

General sewing tips

- For tucks used as a decorative feature, transfer the markings or fold points to the right side of the garment. If the tucks are folded and stitched inside the garment, transfer the markings to the wrong side.
- Unless you are using a commercial pattern (which includes placement marks), make a cardboard template with notches to indicate the tuck depth and the gap between the folds. Note there will be a fold line and a stitching line. With the template placed on the fabric, mark the tuck stitching line and the fold line by cutting tiny notches in the seam allowance or marking with a chalk pencil or tailor's tack. Mark at either end of the tuck to ensure accurate folding. Fold the fabric along the fold line and lap it to the stitching line. Press in place (diagram 1).
- For decorative tucks on the right side, stitch close to the fold on the inside. For tucks on the inside, stitch close to the fold on the right side.
- Pin tucks are usually approximately 1 cm (⅜ in). Wide tucks can be 6–13 mm (¼–½ in).
- For corded tucks, fold the tuck as before and add the cord within the fold on the wrong side of the garment. Working from the right side with a zipper or cording foot, stitch through both fabric layers as close to the cord as possible (diagram 2).

DIAGRAM 2

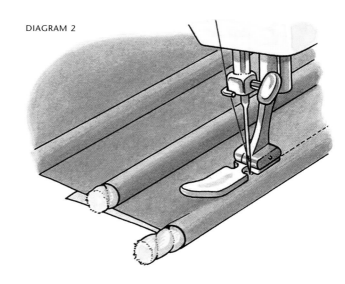

 Helpful hint: *If you are adding tucks to a garment, first tuck the fabric, then cut out to pattern to ensure enough fabric is allowed for each pattern piece and to position tucks where desired (diagram 3).*

DIAGRAM 1

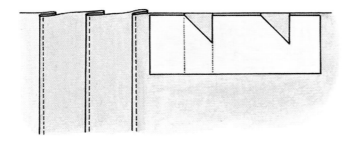

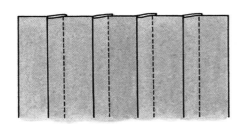

DIAGRAM 3

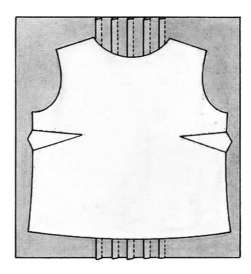

Pleats

As with tucks, there are three main pleat variations

Knife pleats – These are straight pleats, all facing the same direction, lapping right over left.

Box pleats – Made from two pleats, turned away from each other to form a panel.

Inverted pleats – Two straight pleats turned towards each other to form a V opening. Kick pleats are a variation of the inverted pleat and may have the underlay section cut from a contrast fabric to add design detail.

General sewing tips

- As with tucks, unless you are using a commercial pattern, make a template from stiff card, cut to the width of the finished pleat – i.e. 2 cm (¾ in) wide. Mark 'placement line' on one edge and 'fold line' on the other. Use the template to transfer the markings to the fabric, using a different mark for fold and placement lines for easy identification (diagram 4). For unpressed pleats, mark down lines just 5–10 cm (2–4 in) from the top edge. For crisp pressed pleats, mark the whole pleat length.
- Keeping the upper edges even, fold the pleat along the fold line to meet the placement line. Pin and baste in place along the top edge.
- Hem the garment before forming the pleats if possible.
- Always press with a press cloth to avoid leaving fold imprints on the fabric.
- To keep pleats in place, working from the wrong side, machine stitch close to the inner fold, particularly in the hem area (diagram 5).

Helpful hint: Use fusible foldaband on the wrong side for crisp, even pleats.

DIAGRAM 5

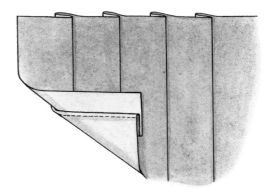

DIAGRAM 4

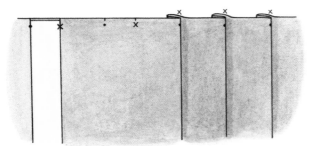

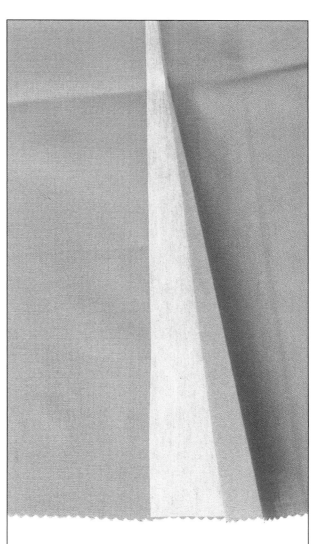

PLEAT WITH FOLDABAND INSIDE

Linings and interlinings

Many garments are lined to give extra body and to help them hang properly. Linings will also cover seams, interfacings etc. They can be made from any lightweight fabric although most are constructed from lining fabric, which is usually nylon or silk. They can be in a matching colour or a striking contrast colour, but do need to be compatible with the main fabric in terms of laundering.

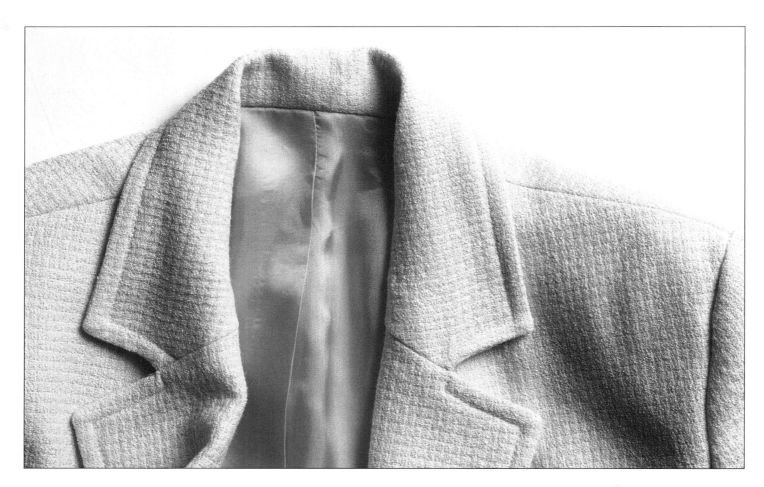

Loose linings

Loose linings use the same pattern pieces as the garment, excluding facings, waistbands, collars and cuffs. They are stitched together in the same manner as the garment before being attached to the garment at the neck, waist etc. before facings are applied. Leave openings for zippers about 2.5 cm (1 in) longer than the zipper placement on the garment.

Having sewn both lining and main garment up to the point of the facings, with wrong sides together, pin the lining to the garment at the neck and front opening on jackets, at the neck and armholes on dresses and at the waist on skirts or trousers. Match seams, darts, notches and raw edges. Baste, then machine stitch along the edges pinned together.

Helpful hint: To allow for wearing ease, reduce the dart size in the back of the jacket lining and then take a pleat at the centre of the neck edge to provide the extra fullness.

Interlinings

Interlinings, also known as underlinings, are another layer, sandwiched between the main fabric and the lining. Interlinings are often sewn with the main fabric as one, adding stability and body to the main fabric. They are cut from the same pattern pieces as the main fabric, excluding facings, collars and cuffs. Transfer the pattern markings to the right side of the interlining and then place the interlining to the fabric, wrong sides together. Baste the layers together around the edges and through the darts etc. Then construct the garment in the usual way, treating the two layers as one.

Zippers

When lining a garment with a zipper, at the zipper area, turn the raw edge of the lining under and slip stitch to the zipper tape (diagram 1).

DIAGRAM 1

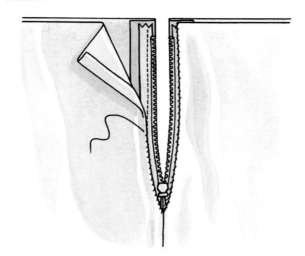

Necklines and armholes

Necklines and armholes are then finished with facings (see Facings and bands, page 62) so that when turned to the inside they encase the raw edges (diagram 2). Finish the waist edge with facing or waistbands (see Waistbands, page 68).

DIAGRAM 2

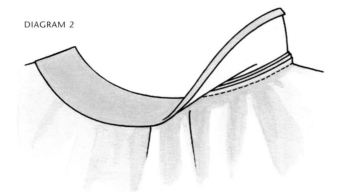

Hems

Turn the lining hem up so that the fold sits just over the stitched hem edge of the garment. Keeping the garment free, tuck the raw edge of the lining to the inside and then machine stitch the hem (diagram 3).

DIAGRAM 3

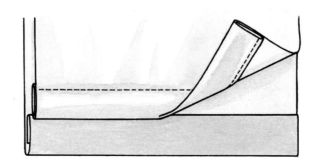

Gathers and ruffles

Fabric is gathered to reduce the length to fit on to a straight edge. Ruffles are gathered pieces of fabric added as a decorative detail. They can be wide or narrow, made from the same or contrasting fabric.

Gathers

1 Use a long basting stitch (the longest stitch available on your sewing machine). Use a contrasting colour thread both in the bobbin and on top so the stitches can easily be removed later.

2 Leave long thread tails at each end of the stitching and stitch within the seam allowance. Pull up using the bobbin thread, adjusting the gathers evenly along the length as you go. If gathering a long edge, divide the length in half and stitch and gather each half at a time. When sewing medium- to heavyweight fabrics, stitch two rows of gathering stitch and pull up both together.

3 Once fully gathered to fit the straight edge, tie off the tails to keep the fabric gathered. Pin with right sides together and machine stitch with the gathered fabric uppermost.

4 Press carefully to avoid crushing the fabric gathers.

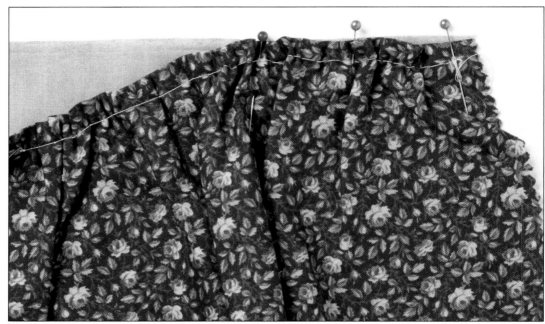

GATHERED EDGE PINNED TO STRAIGHT EDGE

Helpful hint: *When working with very heavyweight fabrics such as furnishings, lay a fine cord along the length and, using a large zigzag stitch, stitch over the cord (avoid stitching through the cord). Anchor the cord at one end with a safety pin and then pull up the cord, adjusting the gathers evenly. Anchor the cord end with a pin to keep the gathers in place until stitched, then remove the cord and keep for later use (diagram 1).*

DIAGRAM 1

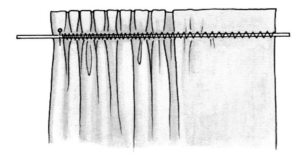

Ruffles

1 To determine the ruffle length, measure the straight edge onto which the ruffle is to be attached. For lightweight fabrics multiply by three. For heavyweight fabrics multiply by one and a half to two.

2 Ruffle depth depends on personal preference, however on children's clothing 2.5–8 cm (1–3 in) works well and on soft furnishings and heavyweight fabric a deeper ruffle of 15–20 cm (6–8 in) is more suitable.

3 Hem ruffle strips before gathering. On lightweight fabrics and stretch fabrics use a rolled or lettuce edge hem (see Hemming, page 58). Alternatively, take a double hem by folding up the hem allowance and tucking the raw edge under again to meet the first fold. Machine stitch in place.

4 If the ruffle is to be added on top of the main fabric and thus both long edges will be visible, hem both before gathering. Hem the top edge with a 1.5 cm (⅝ in) top stitch. Once gathered, pin in position, with the wrong side of the ruffle to the right side of the fabric. Stitch in place, stitching over the previous top stitching (diagram 2).

RUFFLE EXAMPLES

DIAGRAM 2

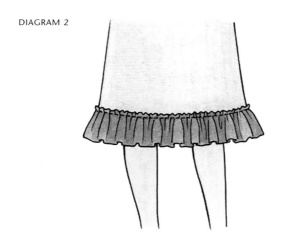

DIAGRAM 3

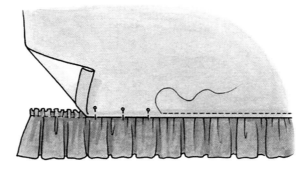

5 When adding a ruffle to a hemline, first reduce the length of the skirt or dress by the depth of ruffle (to avoid lengthening the garment). Do this by cutting off the ruffle depth less 1.5 cm (⅝ in) for the seam allowance. Turn up the raw edge of the garment by the seam allowance and press. Pin the right side of the ruffle to the underside of the garment, matching the raw edge of the ruffle with the turned up edge of the garment. Working from the right side, top stitch in place, stitching close to the garment fold and catching the ruffle in place as you stitch (diagram 3).

Fancy edges

There are many ways to finish edges other than by simply neatening them. These include bias binding and piping in matching or contrasting colours, lace edging and fringing.

Bias binding

Bias binding is made from strips of fabric cut on the bias so that it can curve around corners without puckering, and is folded in half with the long edges tucked in again. One edge is slightly wider than the other (diagram 1). It is used to cover raw edges and provide a decorative trim at the same time. It works well on unlined garments such as edge-to-edge jackets or vests, children's clothes and craft projects, as well as providing a great finish for necklines and armholes. Foldover braid is similar to bias binding, without the tucked under edges. It is used in the same way.

Bias binding can be made in self-fabrics using a bias tape maker (available in various widths) or purchased ready-made, again in different widths and fabric finishes. The choice of binding width depends on the style and fabric to be bound. Lightweight fabrics can be bound with narrow bias binding, whilst heavyweight fabrics need wider bindings to accommodate the bulk of the seam allowances.

If available for your sewing machine, use a bias binding foot through which the tape is fed and wrapped around the fabric edge as you sew. However, it is simple to add the tape without the foot as follows:

BIAS BINDING BEING MADE WITH A BIAS TAPE MAKER

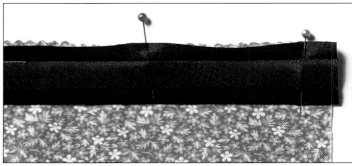

BIAS BINDING BEING STITCHED TO THE FABRIC EDGE

1 Open out the narrowest edge along the side of the bias tape and pin to the garment edge, right sides together. Stitch in place along the crease of the opened out edge.

2 Trim the seam allowance and then fold the tape over to the reverse of the work, encasing the raw edges. Slip stitch in place. Alternatively, stitch in the ditch from the right side, gently pulling the binding and fabric apart to stitch within the previous seam and catching the underside of the bias binding in place.

DIAGRAM 1

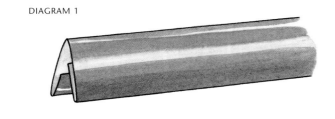

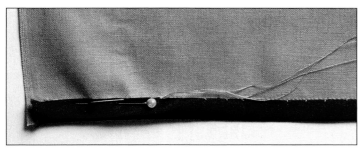

BIAS BOUND FABRIC EDGE

Joining ends

• To join ends, for instance on a neck or armhole, first pin the binding to the edge as before, starting at the centre back or back of armhole. Turn the raw edge of the start of the binding over and pin to hold. Lap the other end over the top of the folded end. Stitch in place (diagram 2). Once the binding is turned to the inside of the garment, the neatened edge will be on the outside.

DIAGRAM 2

Handling corners

• *Outer corners* – Stitch the binding as before, stopping 1.5 cm (⅝ in) from the corner. Fold the binding away from the corner at right angles to make a diagonal fold, pin in place. Then refold along the next edge and start stitching again from where you finished (1.5 cm/⅝ in from the raw edges) (diagram 3).

Fold the binding to the underside as before. A mitre will automatically form on the right side. On the inside, fold the corner into a neat mitre and slip stitch in place.

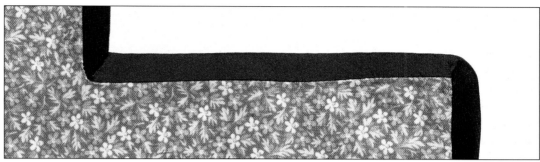

BOUND CORNERS

Slip stitch the rest of the binding as before.

• *Inner corners* – These are handled differently from outer corners. First strengthen the inner corner on the main fabric by stitching 1.5 cm (⅝ in) either side of the corner along the seam line. Clip into the corner, clipping close to the stitching (diagram 4).

Stitch the binding to the fabric as before until you reach the corner. Stop with the needle down and the presser foot raised and open out the fabric beneath the binding at the clipped corner to form a straight line. Continue applying the binding. Bring the corner back together, folding the excess binding diagonally in the corner when turning the binding to the underside. Repeat on the underside, and again tuck the excess into a diagonal fold.

DIAGRAM 3

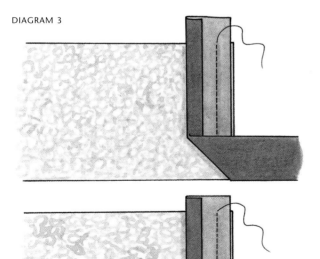

DIAGRAM 4

Piping

Piping is a corded trim, which can be plain cord covered with fabric or decorative cord with a tape that is sewn between the fabric layers so the piping sits on the edge. It is used on soft furnishings and customized clothing. Piping cord varies in thickness, thicker cords being used for heavyweight furnishings and finer cord for fashion.

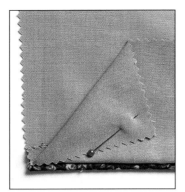

PIPED EDGE

Fabric covered piping – As with bias tape, the fabric to cover piping cord needs to be cut on the bias, approximately 2.5 cm (1 in) wide and as long as required (join lengths if necessary). Fold the strips in half lengthwise, wrong sides together and with the cord sandwiched within the fold, machine stitch the edges together.

Decorative piping – This comes attached to a flange or tape which helps to hold the piping in place by being stitched within the seam allowance. Again, there are different widths of cord for different applications.

General sewing tips

• Use the in-seam method of insertion. Pin the piping to the right side of one piece of the main fabric, matching the raw edge of the fabric and the tape (diagram 5).

• Use a zipper foot to stitch the cord in place.

• Add a second piece of fabric, right sides and edges matching, and then stitch again, stitching as close to the cord as possible. Trim, clip and notch the seam allowances before turning through. The piping is now neatly on the outer edge.

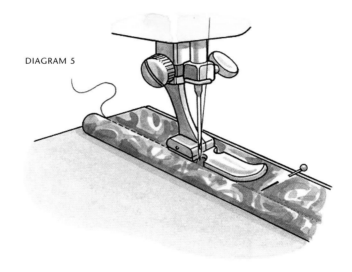

DIAGRAM 5

Overlapping piping ends

Fabric covered piping – Pin the piping to the fabric as above, then where the ends are to overlap, open out the piping fabric and on the under piece, turn the raw end to the inside. Trim the piping cord back 2.5 cm (1 in). Lay the other end of the piping fabric over the first with the cord ends meeting (if desired, hand stitch the cord ends together) (diagram 6). Fold the piping cord again and stitch in place. Add the second layer of fabric as before.

Decorative piping – Start with the piping off the edge of the fabric (starting in an inconspicuous area), curving it on to the seam line and attaching as before. When the piping is to overlap, again curve off the fabric edge over the beginning (diagram 7). It may be necessary to make the last stitches one at a time or by hand as the trim and fabric together are very bulky.

DIAGRAM 6

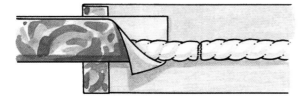

DIAGRAM 7

Surface trims

These are trims that are added to the surface of a project and can be applied by hand or machine. If the trim is over 13 mm (½ in) wide, it is advisable to stitch down both long edges, stitching both in the same direction. Choose a thread that matches the trim.

Mitering at corners

Stitch the trim in place down both long edges, ending the stitching at the seam line at the corner. Fold the trim back on itself and then again along the new stitching line (as for binding corners). Press.

SELECTION OF SURFACE TRIMS

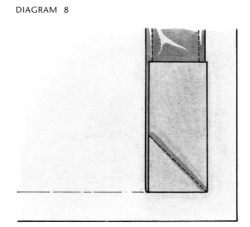

DIAGRAM 8

Unfold the trim so it is just back on itself again and stitch along the diagonal crease (diagram 8). If using a bulky trim, cut away the excess under the diagonal stitching. Fold the trim back along the second placement line again and continue stitching along both long edges.

Beaded trims

Trims with beading are used as decorative embellishment for furnishings, craft projects and fashions. Again the beading is attached to a tape, which can be encased within seam allowances (as piping) or stitched to the surface. If stitched within the seam, remove any beads in the seam allowance by crushing them.

To create curved corners, clip into the tape at the corners, bending it around the corner (diagram 9). Use a zipper foot to stitch close to beading.

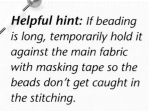

Helpful hint: If beading is long, temporarily hold it against the main fabric with masking tape so the beads don't get caught in the stitching.

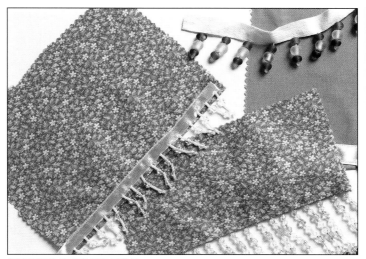

SELECTION OF BEADED TRIMS

DIAGRAM 9

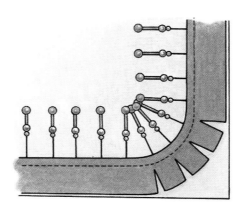

Fringing

As with beaded trims or piping, fringing can be added in-seam if it has a tape attached, or as a surface trim.

Self fringing can also be created by cutting into fabrics that don't fray easily. Decide on the depth of fringe desired and then stitch a guide line. Cut up to this line at even intervals. This type of fringing is ideal on fleece fabrics or bias-cut fabrics that will not unravel.

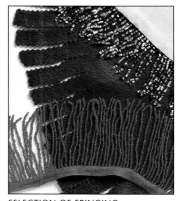

SELECTION OF FRINGING

Elastic and casings

Elastic comes in many widths and styles, each for a different purpose. These include regular straight-edged elastic available in a range of widths, lingerie elastic that can be clear or have decorative edges, fine elastic thread or cord, tubular elastic through which cord can be threaded (for swimwear), buttonhole elastic – with evenly spaced buttonholes, sportswear elastic and waistbanding.

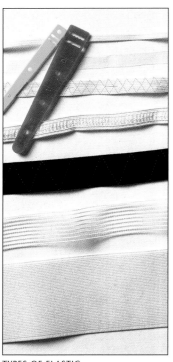

TYPES OF ELASTIC

Elastic can be inserted into a tunnel (casing), applied to the right side of a waist and turned to the inside, or applied at the same time as a casing is formed. Lingerie elastic is designed to be seen and thus is added to the edges.

Easy casings

Used on waists, trouser legs or sleeve hems, casings are created as tunnels through which the elastic is threaded. When cutting out garment sections, remember to add approximately 5 cm (2 in) for the casing (commercial patterns will include an extension to the pattern piece).

1 Having stitched the side seams of the garment, neaten the raw edge of the casing section before turning to the inside. Pin in place and machine stitch close to the inner fold, leaving a gap of about 4 cm (1½ in) for elastic insertion (diagram 1). Stitch around the casing again, this time close to the top fold. Make sure the space between the rows of stitching is wide enough for the width of elastic.

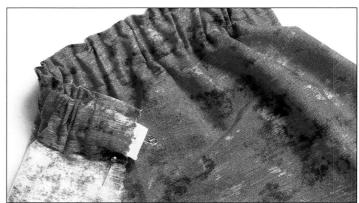

CASING WITH ELASTIC IN

DIAGRAM 1

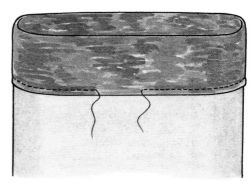

2 Determine the length of the elastic by measuring around the body at waist/sleeve/trouser hem. Subtract 2.5 cm (1 in) from this measurement.

3 Using a safety pin, thread the elastic through the casing and out again at the same place. Overlap the elastic ends and machine stitch them together before allowing them to disappear inside the casing. Before stitching the ends together, pin with a safety pin and try the garment on for size.

Helpful hint: To avoid difficulty feeding elastic through a casing when it comes up against seams, before stitching the casing, use a little fusible hem web to stick the seam allowances down.

Helpful hint: *To prevent the other end of the elastic disappearing inside the casing as you thread it through, anchor it to the garment with another safety pin.*

4 Finish by adjusting the gathers equally and then machine stitching from the top edge to the bottom of the casing at the side seams, centre back and centre front (this will also help prevent the elastic twisting within the casing) (diagram 2).

DIAGRAM 2

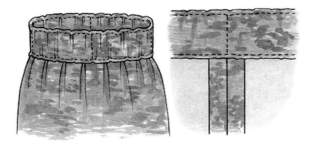

Applied casing

Another form of casing, applied casing is used on dresses at the waist, on shaped edges or on heavyweight fabrics where a self-facing would be too bulky. Usually made from bias binding or seam binding tape, they are attached to the inside of the garment along both long edges. Ensure the two

rows of stitching are far enough apart for the elastic width to sit flat.

To determine the length of bias tape, measure around the ungathered garment. Add 13 mm (½ in) for the seams. Pin in position, overlapping the ends. If necessary tuck the raw edge of the top overlap under. Insert the elastic where the tape overlaps.

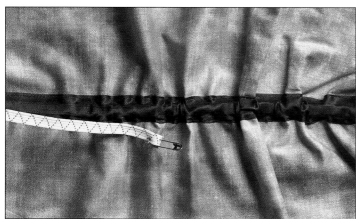

APPLIED CASING

Direct application

Used on shorts, sportswear and knitted garments, the elastic is stitched to the top edge of fabric, which is then folded to the inside to form the casing. It is best applied using the 'quartering' method.

1 Having determined the length of elastic needed, overlap and machine stitch the ends together to form a continuous piece.

2 Neaten the top edge of the fabric and then divide into four equal parts (side seams, centre front and back). Divide the elastic into four equal parts also.

DIAGRAM 3

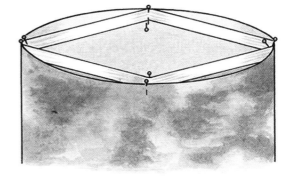

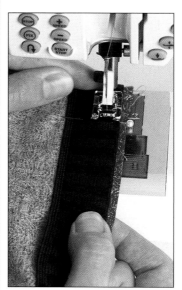

STITCHING ELASTIC WITH ZIGZAG STITCH TO THE WRONG SIDE OF THE TOP EDGE

3 Pin the elastic at the matching quarter marks to the wrong side of the garment with one edge of elastic butted up to the neatened garment edge (diagram 3).

4 Zigzag stitch the elastic to the garment, starting at one quarter mark and stretching the elastic to fit between quarter marks.

5 Fold the garment edge to the inside, taking the elastic with it and again pin in place at the quarter marks. Finish with zigzag stitch through all the layers close to the inner edge, stretching the elastic to fit between the quarters as before.

Lingerie elastic

Designed to be seen, this is applied to the neatened edge of a garment, either on top or underneath the edge, again using the quartering method.

Straps and ties

As the name suggests, straps and ties are used to tie or strap a garment and hold it in position. Straps are wider and ties tend to be narrow. They can be made from self-fabric, contrasting fabric or ribbons and braids.

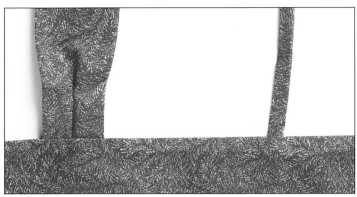

GARMENT TOP WITH STRAPS AND TIES

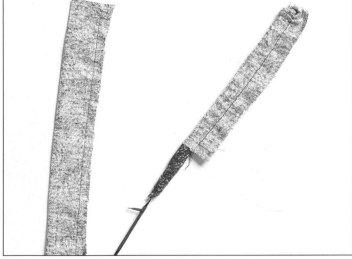

ROULEAU TURNER USED TO TURN TUBING

General sewing tips

- For waist ties, cut fabric strips on the bias to provide extra stretch. For halter neck or shoulder straps, cut fabric on the straight of grain to prevent unwanted stretch.
- Interface straps made of lightweight fabric to add stability.
- Fold the strap or tie in half lengthways, with right sides together and machine stitch the long edge. Turn through to the right side and

reposition the seam at the centre back. Press (diagram 1).
- If you are working with very long straps, machine stitch the short ends and then pivot and stitch the long side, leaving a turning gap in the centre of the long edge. Trim the seam allowances and corners at an angle and turn through. Slip stitch the opening closed.
- To make rounded spaghetti straps, do not trim the seam

allowance after stitching, turn through and allow the seam allowance to fill the tube (diagram 2).
- Use a rouleau turner (long thin needle like tool with fine hook on one end) to turn through very thin ties.
- An alternative method of stitching and turning a strap or tie easily is to use the cord method. Anchor a long cord at one end and sandwich between the folded fabric, with the cord close to the fold. Allow enough cord to leave a 13 cm (5 in) tail. Machine stitch the long edge, without stitching into

the cord. Pull on the cord to pull through the tubing. Cut off the cord and keep for later use (diagram 3).
- Stitch the straps to the right side of the garment prior to adding the facings, matching the end of the strap with the garment edge. Before attaching straps at the back of a garment, pin in place and try the garment on to check the strap length.
- For halter neck ties, simply knot the free end.

DIAGRAM 1

DIAGRAM 2

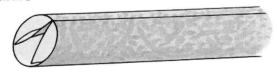

DIAGRAM 3

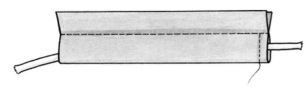

Appliqué

Applying patches or motifs to the fabric surface adds interest, can liven up plain projects or cover worn areas. The term appliqué is used to describe the decorative patches as well as the method of attaching them.

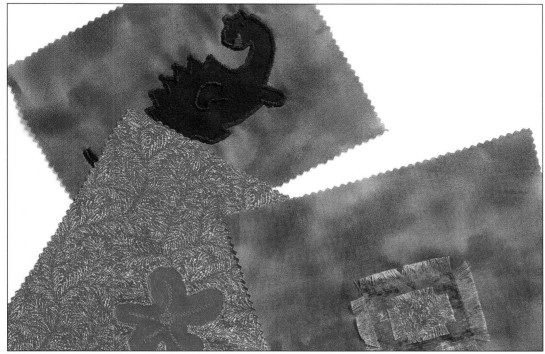

THREE TYPES OF APPLIQUÉ

Often used as a finishing touch, there are different types of appliqué. The most commonly used methods are dealt with here – plain, reverse and raw edge. Others include 'Mola', where multi layers of different coloured fabrics are cut through at different levels to create colourful pictures, and 'Shadow', which involves adding appliqué shapes under layers of sheer fabric.

General sewing tips

- Appliqué shapes can be cut from contrast fabric, from printed motifs on print fabrics or be ready-made. They are usually stitched in place with satin stitch (very close zigzag stitch, width 3, length 0.45), or if appliqué fabric doesn't ravel, use a blanket or straight stitch.
- Keep the motif in position whilst stitching by bonding with fusible web or temporary craft glue.
- If appliquéing onto lightweight fabrics, support the area to prevent the fabric puckering when densely stitched by adding a layer of tearaway stabilizer, which is then torn away once stitching is complete (see Interfacings and stabilizers, page 28).
- When adding lettering or numbers, take care to ensure they are the right way round.

If drawn on the reverse of the appliqué fabric first, they will need to be back to front so when turned over, they are read correctly (diagram 1).
- Stitch slowly to control the direction. The stitch on the right swing of the needle is on the main fabric and the left swing on the appliqué. At curves and corners, stop with the needle down – on inner curves, with the needle in the appliqué; on outer curves, with the needle in the main fabric – then pivot the work slightly before continuing.
- Use a thread colour to match the appliqué. If you are making a multi-layered appliqué, hand baste the different layers in place and then satin stitch the top of visible layers only, again with threads to match the appliqué fabric, unless a contrast is desired (diagram 2).

DIAGRAM 2

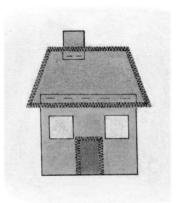

DIAGRAM 1

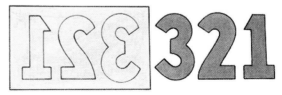

Plain appliqué

This is the most common appliqué technique and is used to create pictures or add motifs. The motifs or components of a picture can be cut from any compatible fabric.

Use paper-backed fusible webbing to anchor the appliqué to the main fabric. First apply the fusible side to the reverse of a piece of appliqué fabric. Then draw around the design and cut out accurately. Remove the paper backing and fuse to the right side of the main garment.

Stitch the appliqué in place using satin stitch, which will also cover the raw edges.

PLAIN APPLIQUÉ

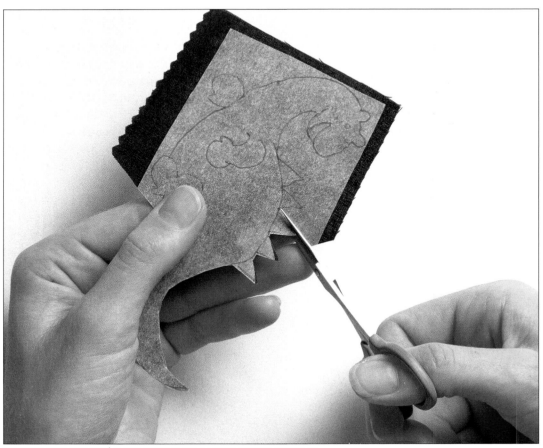

CUTTING OUT APPLIQUÉ FUSED WITH PAPER-BACKED FUSIBLE WEBBING

Raw edge appliqué

As the name suggests, the edges of the applied fabric are left raw to fray and fluff up or be fringed. The appliqué fabric must be cut square or in line with the fabric weave if it is to be fringed (check by pulling thread from the side edges both horizontally and vertically). Fuse the appliqué in place as before, but with fusible web that is 1.5 cm (⅝ in) smaller all around so the edges are not fused. Stitch in place with straight or decorative stitch, 1.5 cm (⅝ in) from the edge. Press and then fringe by pulling out threads from the sides.

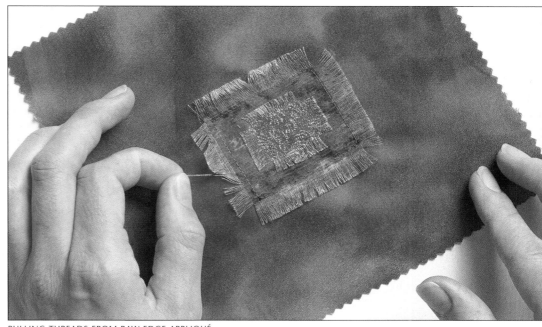

PULLING THREADS FROM RAW EDGE APPLIQUÉ

Helpful hint: Leave the raw edges unfringed and wash repeatedly to get a casual fluffy edge or pink with pinking shears.

Reverse appliqué

The appliqué fabric is applied to the back of the work and then the main fabric is cut away within the design area before being satin stitched around the edges. The result is similar to plain appliqué, but with the motif being lower rather than raised from the main fabric. A combination of the two methods produces a textural 3-D piece of work.

Working on the wrong side of the main fabric, fuse interfacing to the area to be appliquéd. Add the appliqué fabric, right side toward the interfacing. Draw the design on the appliqué fabric in reverse and then straight stitch around the design (diagram 3).

Turn the work to the right side and cut away the main fabric within and close to the stitching. Satin stitch or narrow zigzag stitch around the raw edges. Finish by trimming away the excess appliqué fabric from the reverse of the work.

REVERSE 3-D APPLIQUÉ

DIAGRAM 3

Making curtains and blinds

Sewing for the home has become more and more popular as rooms can be revamped with a selection of easily made curtains and blinds. Using beautiful furnishing fabrics in a range of colours and styles can make all the difference between plain curtains and sumptuous window treatments.

Window treatments

The first consideration is what type of window treatment will suit your room. Is the window large or small? Do you want curtains that are full length, or finish on or just below the windowsill (diagram 1)?

Would a blind be a better option? The hardware is another consideration – curtain tracks or poles? These need to be in place, or the placement marked, before measurements can be accurately taken.

DIAGRAM 1

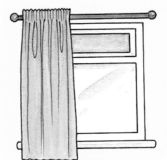

DIAGRAM 2

Calculating fabric amounts

Length

Having decided on the length of curtain – floor length (13 mm/½ in from floor), below sill length (8 cm/3 in below sill), or on sill – take the measurements from the top of the pole or track to the hem length. At the moment this measurement does not include header and hem allowance (diagram 2).

Width

Measure from the outer edges of the brackets on the pole or track. Allow extra width on tracks that overlap at the centre (diagram 2). *Note: if the window is close to the corner of the room also measure from the window to the corner. If less than 20 cm (8 in) there won't be adequate room between the wall and the window to open the curtains properly so consider one curtain hung from the other side.*

Curtain fullness

The amount of fullness is determined by the weight of fabric, as well as the type of header tape. For instance, deep pencil pleats require 3–3½ times fabric width to get the right fullness, whereas goblet-pleated headers need just 2¼ times fabric fullness.

As a general rule: heavy fabrics require a fullness factor of at least 2 to 1; medium-weight fabrics use a fullness factor of 2½ to 1 and lightweight fabrics or voiles look best with at least 3 to 1.

Joining lengths or panels

In order to make up the total width required, it may be necessary to join lengths or panels of fabrics together. When calculating requirements, round up to nearest cm/inch. For instance, if the window is 220 cm (87 in) wide and you want 2¼ times fullness, that is 495 cm (196 in), which will be divided into two curtains of 248 cm (98 in). If the fabric width is 140 cm (54 in), to get the width needed for each curtain will require approximately 1.8 panels joined together for each curtain – rounded up to 2

panels per curtain (which also allows a little for side hems and seams joining panels).

Header tapes, hems and pattern repeats

Other factors to consider before calculating how much fabric is needed include pattern repeat on the chosen fabric, which header tape you wish to use and how deep the hem should be. The pattern repeat is the amount of fabric that a recurring pattern or design on the fabric takes up before it is repeated again (diagram 3). Sometimes you may need to measure the pattern repeat on a length in

the shop; others will note the repeat on the ticket. You will need to add the pattern repeat amount to every length of fabric required to make up the width of each curtain.

Header tape – Add double the depth of the header tape (this can vary from 2.5–20 cm (1–8 in). A goblet header tape is 10 cm (4 in) deep, so 20 cm (8 in) is added to the length. The amount of header tape needed is the same as the overall width, plus 15 cm (6 in) for turnings.

DIAGRAM 3

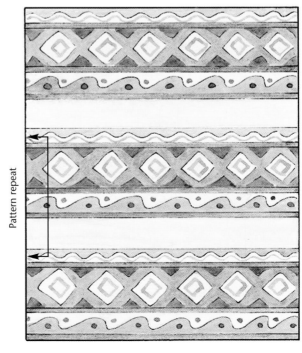

Pattern repeat

Hem allowance – Longer, heavier curtains look better with a wider hem of 10 cm (4 in), lightweight and shorter curtains can have a narrower hem of 5 cm (2 in). Add double the hem depth to each curtain length.

Pattern repeat – As mentioned above, to each length/panel you need to add the pattern repeat of the design on the fabric so that when panels are joined, the pattern matches across the width. For example, a pattern repeat of 33 cm (13 in) needs to be added to each length that makes up one curtain.

To calculate your own requirements complete this simple chart:

Length:
Window length from pole to hem line
Plus header tape depth x 2
Plus hem depth x 2
Plus pattern repeat
= total length per panel

Width:
Window width from pole (outer bracket to outer bracket) plus overlap if curtains overlap
Multiplied by fullness required, i.e. 2, 2½, 3 or 3½ (determined by header type or fabric thickness) =
Divide this by the number of curtains (thus total width per curtain)
Divide this by width of fabric to calculate how many lengths

Linings

Linings add weight to curtains and help them hang better. They also provide added insulation against cold and light, cut down the noise and dust that filters through a window and will give a uniform appearance from the outside.

There are two types of lining: sewn-in (the most commonly used) and loose linings that have a special lining header tape that is attached to the main curtains with hooks. For loose linings you need approximately 1½ times the window width. Sew them in the same way as main curtains.

Sewn-in linings require the same fullness of fabric as the main fabric. The only difference in the calculations is there is no need to add pattern repeat.

Normally curtain lining is white or off-white cotton sateen. However, sheeting, unbleached muslin or pretty cotton prints can also be used. Consider using a pretty cotton if the underside may be visible when curtains are tied back.

Pelmets, valences, swags and jabots

These are treatments for dressing the top of a window that can be used in conjunction with or instead of curtains.

DIAGRAM 4

Pelmets or cornices – These are hardwood boxes, which can be shaped, covered in fabric and trimmed to match the curtains (diagram 4).

DIAGRAM 5

Valances – These are soft fabric toppers like mini curtains, often in a matching or co-ordinating fabric to the main curtains (diagram 5). They can be finished with the same header tape or a more intricate tape. Both pelmets and valances will cover the tops of the curtains.

Swags and jabots – A classic swag is a draping of soft fabric folds used as a top treatment with pleated or gathered side panels. The side panels are the jabots, also known as cascades or tails (diagram 6).

DIAGRAM 6

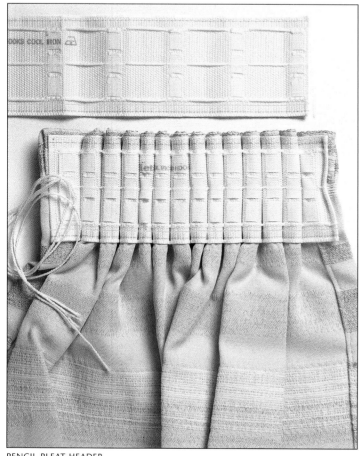

PENCIL PLEAT HEADER

Drapery headers

There are a number of different options to finish the top of curtains. The most common is to add a header tape which is then gathered to form uniform pleats of some sort. Other options include eyelet curtains, tab top and curtains with casings, all of which are threaded onto curtain poles.

Header tapes

These are usually white and have cords attached to the tape in a regular pattern, so that when pulled from one end, the tape and therefore curtain, gathers evenly. There is an extensive range of header tape styles to choose from.

Pencil pleat – Also known as Regis, this is the most popular type of header. For a full effect, you need 2–2½ times the fabric width with this type of tape so that when gathered, it produces evenly spaced pleats across the curtain. It is available in different widths, from narrow tape for lightweight or short curtains and voiles, to deeper tapes, ideal for heavier and full-length curtains. The deeper the tape, the fuller the pleats. Another option is a clear pencil pleat tape designed for transparent fabrics or a mini tape which is used for very lightweight gathers on sheer fabrics.

Pinch pleats – These come in a variety of pinch types, from Tridis to goblet. Tridis pleats are slightly more fanned rather than all even top to bottom, while goblet pleats quite literally resemble a goblet cup. Again the tape is

created with cords, attached along the length so that when pulled up, the tape and curtain pleats in a regular design.

Press 'n' Drape – This is another useful product that is used to attach valances or curtains to unusually shaped frames. One part of the tape has hooks (similar to hook and loop tape) which will then 'hook' on to the special dual purpose header tapes that incorporate the loops (see below).

Dual purpose box pleat – The term dual purpose means it can be used with the Press 'n' Drape window fitting or as a regular tape. The box pleat style provides a very crisp look. Other dual purpose tapes include Trellis and Smocked Pleats – again when cords are pulled up, the header tape gathers into a trellis or smocked style.

Eyelet – Another option is to finish curtains with large eyelets, so that the curtain is threaded onto a pole. The tape is pre-printed with large circular holes or eyelets at even intervals. The tape is attached to the curtain top in the usual way, and then the eyelets are cut from the fabric. To finish off, large two-part rings, available in different metal finishes, are snapped into place front and back of the curtain covering the raw edges of the cut-outs.

Casing curtains – Also known as café curtains, these do not require header tape. Instead, a deep casing is created at the top of the curtain by turning the top edge to the underside, and stitching from side edge to side edge, approximately 8 cm (3 in)

105

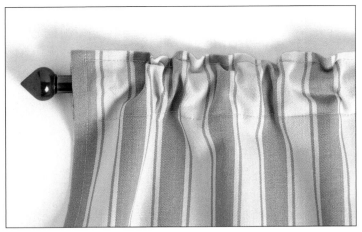

CASING CURTAIN

WEIGHTS

from the top and then again, 2.5 cm (1 in) from the top. The curtain is then slipped onto a rod (which is concealed within the casing). The amount of fabric width needed for this type of curtain depends on the length of the curtain, but can be as little as 1½ widths.

Tab top curtains – These curtains have fabric strips that are looped over a pole and attached to the curtain top by machine stitching or using buttons or clips. The width and intervals between the tab tops depends on curtain weight and length, the longer and heavier the curtains, the wider and closer the tabs need to be (to prevent the

curtain sagging in between the tabs). As a guide, allow a gap of half the finished tab width between each tab. This type of curtain doesn't use as much fabric as curtains with headers as they are not usually gathered and thus are the width of the window plus turnings. The curtain top needs to be held above the window frame, so the pole may need to be positioned slightly higher than usual.

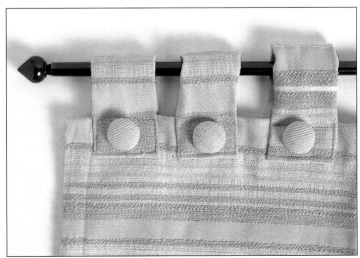

TAB TOP CURTAIN

Adding weights

Hem weights are added to improve the hang of curtains, to give weight to the bottom, which in turn helps them hang straight. There are two main types of weight – a series of little lead pellets that are encased in a net tape and round button-shaped discs that may have holes for sewing weights in place.

Lead tape – Lay the tape in the fold of the hem allowance, catch stitching it in place at the sides of the curtain.

Lead discs – Either stitch to the inside of the lining using the buttonholes or make little bags to hold the weights. To make the bags, simply cut a rectangle of fabric approximately 13 mm (½ in) wider than the disc by four times the disc size. Fold the fabric into thirds lengthways, overlapping the centre and then stitch the side seams together. Push the disc into the little bag and attach to the lining hem. Depending on the weight and length of the curtains, attach discs either side or at intervals along the curtain bottom.

Blinds

There are three main types of blind – Roman, Austrian and roller blind. Blinds can be used instead of, or as well as curtains to dress a window. All will cover part of the window when up and thus may block a little light.

Roman blinds – This is the most common type of blind, which, when pulled up by drawstring cords, folds into neat, evenly spaced concertina folds held in place by rods inserted into pockets at the back of the blind (diagram 7). Longer blinds may have three or four centre pleats whilst smaller windows need just one or two. Each window will vary depending on the overall depth.

Helpful hint: Make the top pleat deeper and bottom pleat half width and the blind will fold up into even equal pleats every time.

Austrian blinds – These are also pulled up by a cord system attached to the reverse of the blind. Preferably they should hang below a windowsill by about 25 cm (10 in) and the fabric needs to be twice the width of the batten, to which the blind is fixed at the top, to create the fullness. When down they look a bit like curtains, when up, they gather into puffy swags (diagram 8). A lightweight fabric creates the best type of folds.

Roller blinds – These are the simplest style, with fabric rolled up onto a roller by a cord and sprocket system (diagram 9). Add an extra 20 cm (8 in) to the length so that there is some fabric on the roller when the blind is down. As the overall width of the roller itself is 3.5 cm (1½ in) wider than the fabric, make sure the fabric covers the glass completely.

DIAGRAM 10

DIAGRAM 7

DIAGRAM 8

DIAGRAM 9

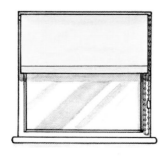

Measuring for blinds

As blinds need to fit a window snugly, the first task is to measure accurately. The decision of whether to mount within the recess or outside depends on blind style, personal choice and window openings (diagram 10).
Width – If the blind is to fit inside the recess, measure from side edge to side edge of the inner window frame. If it is to fit outside the recess, measure at least 8 cm (3 in) beyond the outer window frame to make sure the blind fully covers the recess. Measure the width at the top and bottom of the window in case it is not perfectly square or rectangular. Note: when fitting a blind inside the recess, attach the blind hardware at least 5 cm (2 in) in from the glass to prevent condensation damaging the blind.
Length – If the blind is to fit inside the recess, measure from the top of the hardware (wooden batten) to the sill. If it is to fit outside the recess,

again measure from the top of the wooden batten to at least 5 cm (2 in) below the sill (or 25 cm/10 in for Austrian blinds).

Fabric required

Add 5 cm (2 in) for seam allowances and hems to the window width measurement and 9 cm (3½ in) to the length. If necessary, join fabric widths to get the full width. For Austrian blinds, allow double the window width for the blind to gather effectively.

Both Austrian and Roman blinds also require lots of cording, blind tape, rod pockets etc. The amount required will depend on the size of the blind. Kits are available which include all components, alternatively commercial patterns for blinds include details on how to measure and calculate requirements as well as a list all the components needed.

Projects

Dressing up tunic

Children love to dress up – for Halloween, holidays or simply for fun. This easy tunic is quick to make and can be used as the basis for a multitude of costumes – from Mary to Captain Hook!

TO FIT AGE 4–8

MATERIALS

2 m (2 yd) of 90 cm (36 in) wide cotton mix fabric or 1 m (1 yd) of 150 cm (60 in) wide

25 cm (¼ yd) of 112 cm (45 in) wide cotton for belt

Remnants of braids/trims and buttons

Small plate

Bias binding maker

Marking pen/chalk

Bias binding for neck edge (optional)

DIAGRAM 1

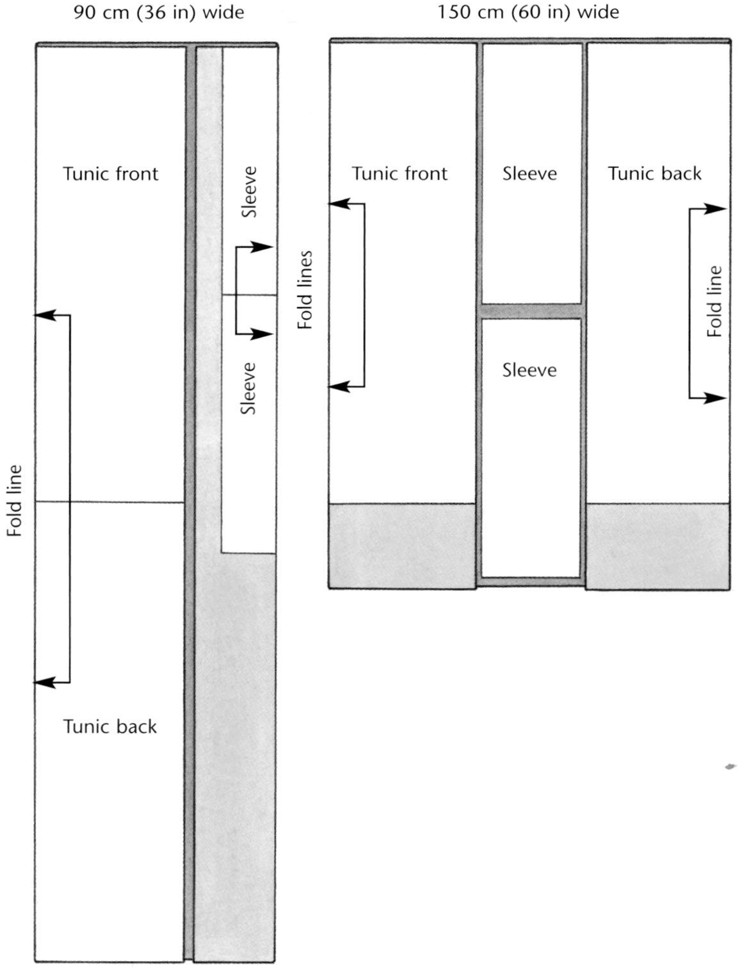

90 cm (36 in) wide   150 cm (60 in) wide

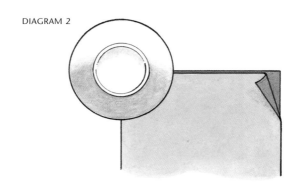

Cutting out

- Fold the main fabric lengthwise as shown and mark out the garment sections to cut on the fold as follows:
- For the tunic, mark and cut out two rectangles 27 x 90 cm (10¼ x 35½ in).
- For the sleeves, cut two rectangles 10 x 50 cm (4 x 20 in) wide. If using 150 cm (60 in) wide fabric, cut the sleeves on a single layer 20 x 50 cm (8 x 20 in) (diagram 1).
- From remnants, cut bias strips 5 cm (2 in) wide to use to bind the neck edge.

Sewing

1 Use the plate to draw a curve at the neck edge of the folded front and back, placing it so approximately a quarter of the plate is on the fabric (diagram 2). Cut off the fabric outside the curve line.

DIAGRAM 2

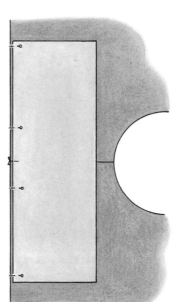

DIAGRAM 3

2 Stitch the front to the back at the shoulder seams. Press.

3 Open out the front/back and, finding the middle of the long edge on the sleeve, pin to the shoulder seam of the tunic, right sides together (diagram 3). Pin the rest of the sleeve edge to the back and front respectively. Sew in place.

*Variation
see page 112*

4 Pin then stitch the front to the back from the sleeve edge to the tunic hem, pivoting at the underarm seam. If you are sewing the tunic for a pirate, leave side slits in the tunic: stitch the side seams from the sleeve to half the side length. Press the seam allowances open and neaten, neatening all of the seam allowance. Top stitch the slit from the right side, catching the seam allowance in the stitching. Use the needle in the centre position and the right edge of presser foot as a stitch guide.

5 Hem the tunic and sleeves with a narrow double hem – turn the raw edge under 1 cm (⅜ in) then again, tucking the raw edge in to meet the first fold. Machine stitch in place.

6 If desired, machine stitch trims 8 cm (3 in) from the tunic and sleeve hem edge.

Helpful hint: For angels, fairies, scarecrows etc., cut a jagged hem with pinking shears rather than machine hemming.

7 Sew bias strips together to make enough to go around the neck edge. Make into bias binding using the binder maker (see page 92). Alternatively, use purchased bias binding. Unfold one edge of bias tape and pin, right sides together, to the neck edge, starting at the centre back (diagram 4). Pin and baste all around. Machine stitch in position.

DIAGRAM 4

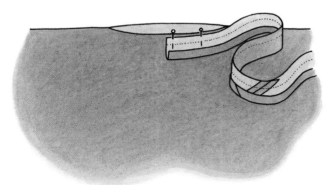

8 Clip the seam allowance of the garment and then turn the bias tape to the wrong side, encasing the raw edges.

9 Slip stitch the bias binding over the seam inside the garment, or working from the right side, stitch in the ditch, catching the tape on the underside in the stitching. (To stitch in the ditch, spread seam open and stitch along the previous stitching).

10 To make the belt, fold the long ends in to the centre, overlapping slightly. Tuck the raw edge of the overlap under and press. Machine stitch in place down the centre of the belt. If desired, stitch again in parallel rows for added strength (diagram 5). Hem the short ends of the belt.

DIAGRAM 5

Variations

Adapt the tunic to make costumes for angels, shepherds, kings and even a Peter Pan, witch or wizard. Choose fabric colours to suit the character. Layer with a long or short vest (the same pattern as the tunic, with the front cut down the centre). Add head shawls or scarves to finish the costume.

Fabric quantities:

Long vest or short tunic – 75 cm (1 yd) of 150 cm (60 in) wide printed cotton

Short vest – 80 cm (⅞ yd) of 150 cm (60 in) wide fur/texture fabric

Head shawl – 50 cm (½ yd) of 150 cm (60 in) wide polycotton

- For a short tunic cut two rectangles on the fold, each 27 x 64 cm (10½ x 25¼ in). Sew as for main tunic.
- For a long vest, cut two rectangles as for the short tunic. Cut the neck edges as before, then cut down the centre front. Neaten the front, hem and sleeve edges with a double hem.
- For a short vest, cut two rectangles on the fold, each 27 x 30 cm (10½ x 12 in). Cut the edge as before then cut the front piece in half down the centre.
- For head coverings, neaten the raw edges by simply pinking with pinking shears. Wear with cord or a fabric strip tied around the crown of the head.

Costume tips

Head shawl – for Mary, place shawl on head, centring long edges evenly at sides, then wrap the edges over the opposite shoulders so they hang down the back. For Joseph and shepherds, again place on head with long edges evenly at sides, then wrap rope around the head and tie at the back.
Crowns – make from gold card, tinsel and jewels or buttons glued in place.
Angel wings – make them from A2 gold card, threaded with 2.5 m (3 yd) of narrow silver ribbon.
Halo – tie gold or silver tinsel around the child's head.

Edge-to-edge jacket

This easy-make, easy-wear jacket is a classic box shape. Made in a soft medium-weight tweed, it is fastened at the front with decorative hook fastenings.

Materials

160 cm (1¾ yd) of 150 cm (60 in) wide novelty tweed, suiting or medium-weight fabric, plus lining fabric

OR 185 cm (2 yd) of 115 cm (45 in wide)

60 x 10 cm (24 x 4 in) wide medium-weight fusible interfacing

2 reels polyester thread

1 m (1 yd) lacing, cord or ribbon or hook fastenings (optional)

Cutting out

- Copy the pattern on page 119 onto pattern drafting paper, following the lines corresponding to your size and the cutting lines for the Jacket. Alternatively, enlarge the pattern on a photocopier. Transfer all pattern markings to the paper.
- Fold the fabric in half lengthwise and lay out the pattern for the fabric width chosen (diagrams 1 and 1a), placing the back and collar on the fold and the side front, front and sleeve with the straight of grain line parallel with the selvages. Cut out, cutting around the notches. Use the collar pattern to cut a second collar piece.

DIAGRAMS 1 AND 1A

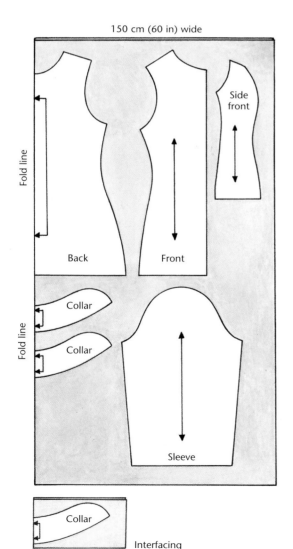

150 cm (60 in) wide

Fold line

Fold line

Back

Front

Side front

Collar

Collar

Sleeve

Collar

Interfacing

115 cm (45 in) wide

Fold line

Fold line

Back

Front

Collar

Collar

Side front

Sleeve

• Use the same pattern pieces to cut out lining in the same way, excluding the collar.
• Use the collar pattern to cut one in interfacing, again placing the pattern on the fold.

Sewing

1 Ease stitch the curved side of the front side section by stitching with a 3.5 mm (⅛ in) stitch length just inside the seam allowance. Take the side fronts and main fronts and place right sides together, matching the notches and gently easing the side front section around the curves of the centre front section. Pin and sew. Press the seams open.

2 Pin the fronts to the back at the shoulder and side seams. Machine stitch the seams, neaten the edges, then press the seams open.

3 Ease stitch around the top curved end of the sleeve by stitching with a 3.5 mm (⅛ in) stitch length close to the seam line – 13 mm (½ in) from the raw edge. Fold the sleeves in half lengthwise, right sides together and sew the underarm seam. Press open the seam allowances and neaten with overcast or zigzag stitch. Alternatively bind the raw seam allowance edges using bias tricot tape (see Bound seams, page 55).

4 Turn the sleeves right way out, slip into the armhole so that the centre of the eased top matches the shoulder seam and the underarm seams match. Pin and baste into place so the right side of the sleeve faces the right side of the jacket. Machine stitch the sleeve in place (diagram 2).

DIAGRAM 2

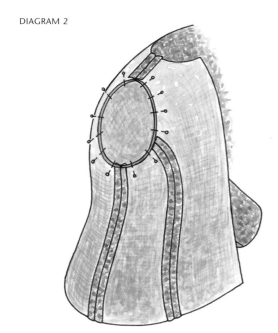

5 Repeat steps 1 to 4 for the lining.

6 Mark the centre on one collar section and the centre of the back. With right sides together, pin and baste the collar around the neckline of the garment, matching the centre points marked. Sew the seam then clip one side of the seam allowance to reduce some of the bulk.

7 Interface the other collar section by fusing interfacing to the wrong side. Allow to cool before handling, then attach to the lining neckline, with right sides together and matching centre points. Sew the seam and clip seam allowance of main fabric to reduce bulk.

8 With right sides together, place the lining of the jacket to the main fabric of the jacket, matching all seams and the collar. Pin and baste the centre fronts and around the collar.

9 Sew around the collar, pushing the neck seam down out of the way as you do so. Stop and fix stitch or back stitch to secure.

10 Sew down both centre front seams, pushing the neck seam up out of the way as you do so.

11 Clip around the collar every 2.5 cm (1 in) and grade the seams to reduce bulk. Layer seam the allowances: cut one to 1 cm (⅜ in) and the other to 6 mm (¼ in).

12 Turn the jacket to the right side and press, ensuring the seams run along the edge. Once pressed, top stitch up the left centre front, around the collar then down the right centre front.

13 Trim the lining hem by 2.5 cm (1 in). Make a double hem in the garment by turning the main fabric up 13 mm (½ in) and again by 2.5 cm (1 in), encasing the raw edge of the lining. Hand blind stitch or top stitch in place. Hem the cuffs in the same way.

14 Hand stitch the fastenings to the jacket front.

Helpful hint: *If you are using a fabric that frays easily, dab a little fabric glue on the cut seam allowance of the collar where it meets the garment.*

Simple shell top

This simple yet classic sleeveless top in pretty broderie anglaise has a zipper at the back and is fully lined. Team it with suits or separates for office or casual wear.

Materials

1 m (1 yd) of 150 cm (60 in) wide lightweight cotton broderie anglaise and lining fabric

OR 1 m (1 yd) of 115 cm (45 in) wide

36-cm (14-in) nylon zipper

2 reels of polyester thread

Cutting out

- Copy the pattern on page 119 onto pattern drafting paper, following the lines corresponding to your size and the cutting lines for the Shell Top. Alternatively, enlarge the pattern on a photocopier. Transfer all pattern markings to the paper.
- Fold the fabric in half lengthwise and lay out the pattern for the fabric width chosen (diagrams 1 and 1a), placing the front on the fold and the back and side front with the straight of grain line parallel with the selvages. Cut out, cutting around the notches. Transfer all markings for darts etc. to the wrong side of the fabric.
- Use the same pattern pieces to cut out lining in the same way.

DIAGRAM 1

150 cm (60 in) wide

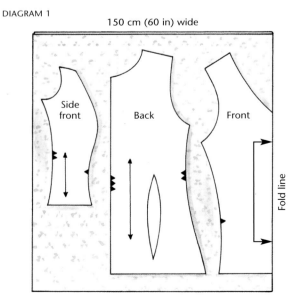

DIAGRAM 1A   115 cm (45 in) wide

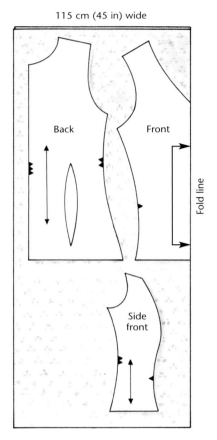

Sewing

1 Ease stitch the inner (curved) seam of the front side sections. To do this increase the stitch length to 3 mm (⅛ in) and, if necessary, slightly loosen the needle tension so that the fabric gathers very, very slightly. Stitch within the seam allowance, close to the seam line.

2 Pin the eased seam of the side front, right sides together to the centre front section, matching the notches. Machine stitch in place. Press the seams open (diagram 2).

DIAGRAM 2

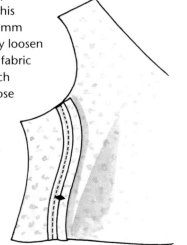

3 On the back pieces, fold, baste then sew the waist darts, starting at the tapered point and stitching to the other point. Press the darts toward the side seams.

4 With right sides together, pin the back pieces together to form the centre back seam. Baste down the seam line. Press open the seam and then insert a centred zipper (see page 76).

5 Join the lining side fronts and the centre front pieces together as in steps 1–2 above.

6 With right sides together, join the front to the back at the shoulder seams. Press the seams open. Repeat for the lining front and back. Stitch the darts in the lining as in step 3 above.

DIAGRAM 3

DIAGRAM 4

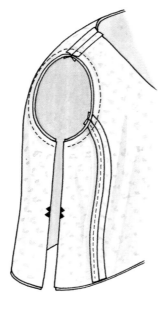

7 Pin the lining to the main fabric, right sides together, matching all seams, pinning at the neck edge and armholes. Baste the armholes (diagram 3).

8 Machine stitch around the armholes (diagram 4). Grade the seam allowances by layering them, cutting the main fabric to 1 cm (⅜ in) and the lining fabric to 6 mm (¼ in). Clip into the seam allowances every 2.5 cm (1 in) then turn through and press the armholes, ensuring the seam runs along the edge.

9 Trim 1 cm (⅜ in) from the lining hem edge.

10 Open out again to separate the lining from the main fabric and then with right sides together, match up the underarm seams. Pin and baste the side seams of the lining and then the main fabric. Starting at the hem, sew up the lining side seam then over the underarm seam, then down the side seam of the main fabric. Neaten the seam allowances and press. Turn the lining to the inside (diagram 5).

DIAGRAM 5

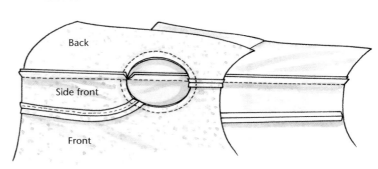

11 Pin the lining and the outer fabric together at the hem.

12 Hem the main fabric by turning under 6 mm (¼ in), then again by 1 cm (⅜ in), covering the raw edge of the lining fabric. Pin and then top stitch in place.

13 On the main fabric, clip the seam allowance at the centre front by 1.5 cm (⅝ in) then turn the seam allowance to the wrong side by this amount around the entire neck edge. Repeat for the lining fabric.

14 Pin and baste the lining to the main fabric, sandwiching the raw edges between the two layers. Edge stitch 3 mm (⅛ in) from the edge.

15 Finally turn under the centre back seam on the lining and hand stitch to the zipper tape.

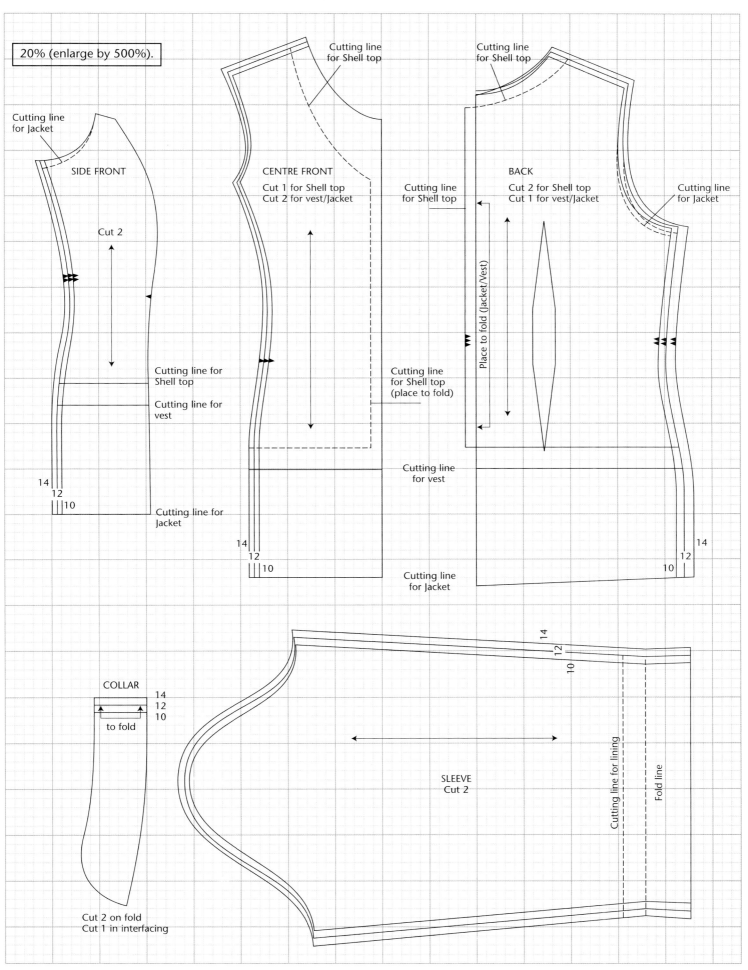

20% (enlarge by 500%).

Cutting line
for Jacket

SIDE FRONT

Cut 2

Cutting line for
Shell top

Cutting line for
vest

14
12
10

Cutting line for
Jacket

Cutting line
for Shell top

CENTRE FRONT
Cut 1 for Shell top
Cut 2 for vest/Jacket

Cutting line
for Shell top

Cutting line
for Shell top
(place to fold)

14
12
10

Cutting line
for Shell top

BACK
Cut 2 for Shell top
Cut 1 for vest/Jacket

Cutting line
for Jacket

Place to fold (Jacket/Vest)

Cutting line
for vest

14
12
10

Cutting line
for Jacket

COLLAR
14
12
10
to fold

Cut 2 on fold
Cut 1 in interfacing

14
12
10

SLEEVE
Cut 2

Cutting line for lining

Fold line

Fleece vest

A great little bodywarmer, this unisex vest is easy to sew in funky fleece. It's also fast to make because fleece doesn't ravel which means that the seams don't need extra neatening.

Materials

1 m (1 yd) of 150 cm (60 in) fleece
OR 1 m (1 yd) of 115 cm (45 in)
46-cm (18-in) open-ended nylon zipper
3 m (3¼ yd) of 2.5 cm (1 in) wide stretch bias binding
1 reel polyester thread

Cutting out

- Copy the pattern on page 119 onto pattern drafting paper, following the lines corresponding to your size and the cutting lines for the vest. Alternatively, enlarge the pattern on a photocopier. Transfer all pattern markings to the paper.
- Fold the fabric in half lengthwise and lay out the pattern as shown in diagrams 1 and 1a, following the diagram for your fabric width. Place the back on the fold and the front and side front with the straight of grain line parallel with the selvages. Cut out, cutting around the notches.

Sewing

1 Ease stitch the inner (curved) seam of the front side sections To do this increase the stitch length to 4 mm (³⁄₁₆ in) and, if necessary, slightly the loosen needle tension so that the fabric gathers very, very slightly. Stitch within the seam allowance, close to the seam line.

2 Pin the eased seam of the side front, right sides together, to the centre front section, matching the notches. Machine stitch in place. Press the seams open (diagram 2).

3 With right sides together, hand baste the centre fronts together. Press the seam open. Insert the zipper (see page 76).

4 On the back pieces, fold, baste then sew the waist darts, starting at the tapered point and stitching to the other point. Press the dart toward the side seams.

5 With right sides together, sew the shoulder seams and side seams. Press the seams open.

DIAGRAMS 1 AND 1A

115 cm (45 in) wide

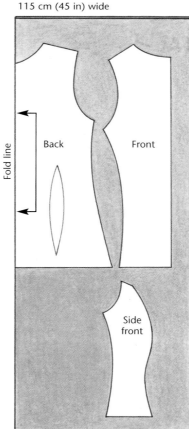

150 cm (60 in) wide

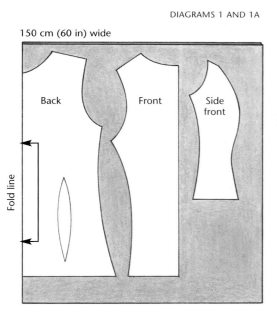

DIAGRAM 2

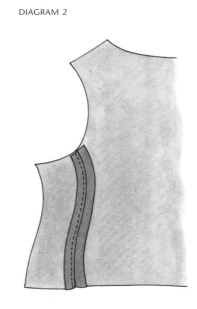

6 Open out the stretch bias binding, pin and baste, right sides together, around the armholes, overlapping the ends close to the underarm. Sew in place 6 mm (¼ in) from the edge (diagram 3). Turn the binding to the inside of garment, encasing the raw fleece edge and making sure the seam runs along the edge. Pin and baste in place then stitch in the ditch from the right side, catching the underside in the stitching (see Machine stitching, page 46). Repeat for the neck, front and hem edges.

DIAGRAM 3

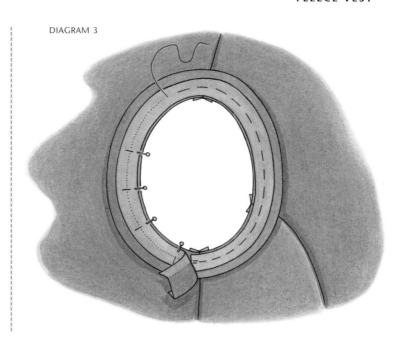

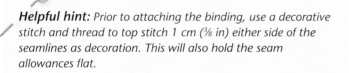

Helpful hint: *Prior to attaching the binding, use a decorative stitch and thread to top stitch 1 cm (⅜ in) either side of the seamlines as decoration. This will also hold the seam allowances flat.*

Timeless trousers

Cool linen trousers are a wardrobe must-have for summer.
This pair has a faced waist, side zipper and side pocket.

Materials

170 cm (2 yd) of 150 cm (60 in) wide medium-weight linen or cotton fabric

1 m (1 yd) x 10 cm (4 in) fusible interfacing

18-cm (7-in) nylon zipper

1 reel matching polyester thread

Chalk pencil (optional)

Cutting out

- Copy the pattern on page 125 onto pattern drafting paper, following the lines corresponding to your size and the cutting lines for the Trousers. Alternatively, enlarge the pattern on a photocopier. Transfer all pattern markings to the paper.
- Fold the fabric selvages into the centre, right sides together. Lay out the pattern as shown in diagram 1, placing the facings on the folds and the trouser front, back and pocket with the straight of grain line parallel with the selvages. Cut out, cutting around the notches.

DIAGRAM 1

150 cm (60 in) wide

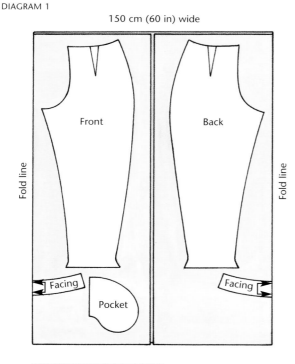

Interfacing

Helpful hint: If it is difficult to tell right from wrong side of the fabric, before removing the pattern, mark the wrong side of the fabric with chalk pencil to indicate which side is which (to ensure there will be a left and right trouser leg).

Sewing

1 Fold out, pin and stitch the darts in the front and back trouser pieces, stitching from the tapered point to the widest part at the waist. Press the darts towards the side seams.

2 Take a left back and left front leg piece (in wear) and place with right sides together, matching the notches. Pin and baste the inside and outside seams. Sew the full length of the inside seam (diagram 2).

DIAGRAM 2

3 On the outside seam match the top of the zipper to the waistline. Measure down the length of the zipper and mark with a pin. Sew from the pin on the outside seam down to the hem.

4 Press open the seams and insert a lapped zipper (see page 77).

5 Take the right-hand front and back legs (in wear) and match the straight section on the pockets to the side seams. Match the O marking on the bottom of the pocket to the side seam and the top of the pocket to the waistline. Pin and baste into place. Sew the pocket to the leg pieces down the side seam only (diagram 3).

DIAGRAM 3

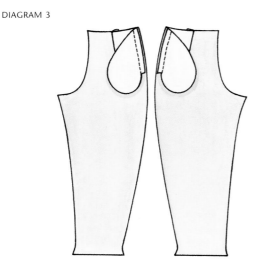

6 Open out the pocket bags and press. Place the front and back of the right legs together, right sides together. Pin and baste around the pocket and down the side seam (diagram 4). Machine stitch the seam. Neaten with overcast or zigzag stitch.

DIAGRAM 4

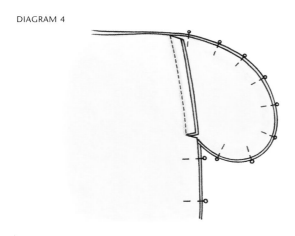

7 Pin and stitch the inside leg seam. Again, neaten the raw edges with overcast or zigzag stitch.

8 Baste the pocket to the front of the trousers, ensuring it lays flat.

9 Turn the trouser legs inside out and then insert one leg into the other, right sides together, so the curved front, back and inside leg crotch seams match. Pin then stitch from the centre front to the centre back, working slowly around the curved crotch area (diagram 5). Reinforce the stitch around the crotch with another line of straight stitching. Clip the seams and neaten with narrow zigzag stitch or overcast stitch. Press.

DIAGRAM 5

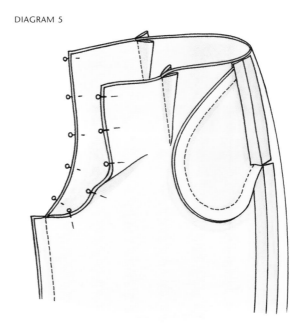

10 Attach interfacing to the wrong sides of the front and back facings. Once cool, place the facings right sides together and sew right side (in wear) short ends together to make one continuous facing. Press the seam open.

11 With trousers right side out, place the facing, right sides together, to the waistline, matching the seam in the facing with right seam (and pocket) on the trousers. Sew around the waist, ensuring the top of the pocket is caught in the stitching. Grade the seam allowance, trimming each layer of allowance a different width to layer them and reduce bulk.

12 Neaten the other long edge of the facing with zigzag stitch or overcast stitch. Press. Turn the facing to the inside, with the seam on the edge. Tuck the raw edges of the open ends under and press. Slip stitch the facing ends to the zipper tape. Finish the waist with edge stitching, working from the right side and stitching a scant 3 mm (⅛) in from the edge.

13 Neaten the raw edge of the hems then turn up the hem allowance to the length desired. Blind hem stitch in place (see page 43).

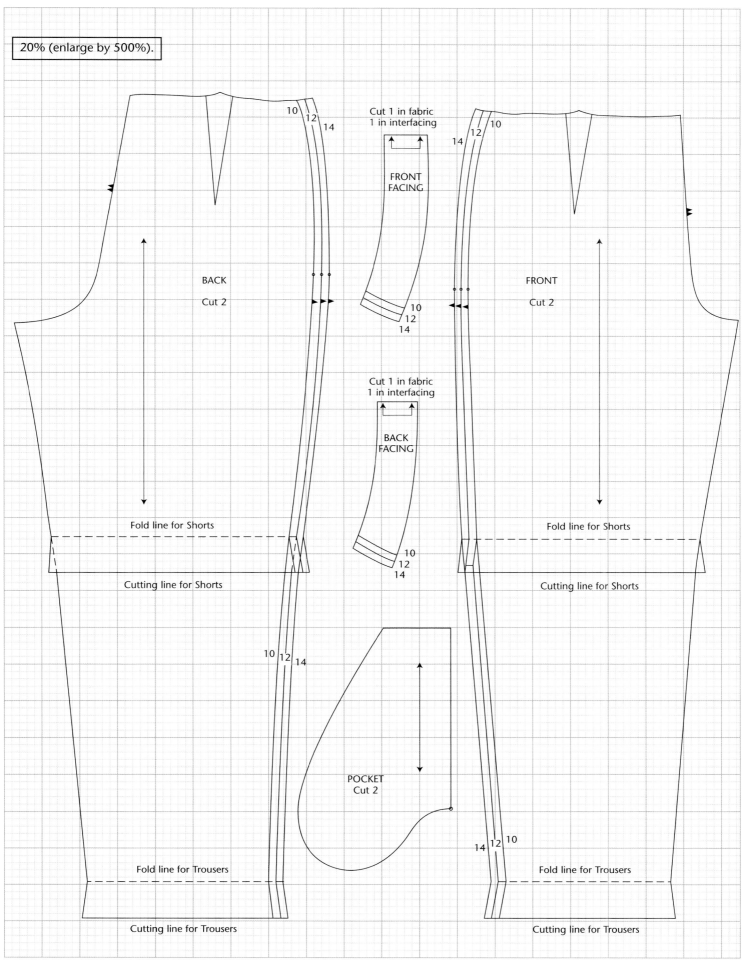

20% (enlarge by 500%).

Cut 1 in fabric
1 in interfacing

FRONT
FACING

10
12
14

Cut 1 in fabric
1 in interfacing

BACK
FACING

10
12
14

10
12
14

BACK
Cut 2

FRONT
Cut 2

14 12 10

Fold line for Shorts

Fold line for Shorts

Cutting line for Shorts

Cutting line for Shorts

10 12 14

POCKET
Cut 2

14 12 10

Fold line for Trousers

Fold line for Trousers

Cutting line for Trousers

Cutting line for Trousers

Casual shorts

Adapted from the trouser pattern, these comfortable casual shorts look good with a lightweight jacket or simple top.

Materials

1 m (1 yd) of 150 cm (60 in) wide linen-look, cotton or denim fabric
1 m (1 yd) of 10 cm (4 in) wide fusible interfacing
18-cm (7-in) nylon zipper
1 reel polyester thread

Cutting out

- Copy the pattern on page 125 onto pattern drafting paper, following the lines corresponding to your size and the cutting lines for the Shorts. Alternatively, enlarge the pattern on a photocopier. Transfer all pattern markings to the paper.
- Fold the fabric selvages into the the centre, right sides together, and lay out the pattern as shown in diagram 1, placing the facings on the folds and the front and back with the straight of grain line parallel with the selvages. Cut out, cutting around the notches.

DIAGRAM 1

150 cm (60 in) wide

Helpful hint: If it is difficult to tell right from wrong side of fabric, before removing pattern, mark wrong side of fabric with chalk pencil to indicate which side is which (to ensure there will be a left and right leg).

Sewing

1 Fold out, pin and stitch the darts in the front and back pieces, stitching from the tapered point to the widest part at the waist. Press the darts toward the side seams.

2 Follow steps 2–5 from Timeless trousers on page 122 to complete the left leg of the shorts.

3 Take the right-hand side leg pieces (in wear) and place right sides together. Pin and stitch the outside leg seam and then the inside leg seam. Neaten the raw edges with overcast or zigzag stitch. Press.

4 Turn the shorts inside out and slip one leg inside the other leg so the right sides of the fabric are together. Match the side seams, the centre back and front of the crotch seam. Sew from front to back. Reinforce the stitch around the crotch area, then neaten the seam allowance and clip. Press.

5 Attach the waist facing and hem as for the Timeless trousers, steps 11–14.

Classic bustier

Bustiers are timeless garments, great for day- or eveningwear. This easy pattern is interfaced, boned and lined and made in pretty embroidered silk.

Materials

1 m (1 yd) of 115 cm (45 in) wide silk, satin, brocade or dupion fabric

1 m (1 yd) of 115 cm (45 in) wide matching lining fabric

1 m (1 yd) of lightweight woven interfacing

Dressmaker's chalk

2 reels of matching thread

Size 80 sewing machine needle

1.5 m (1½ yd) boning

25-cm (10-in) separating zipper

Hook and eye (optional)

Cutting out

- Copy the pattern on page 131 onto pattern drafting paper, following the lines to correspond to your size. Alternatively, enlarge the pattern on a photocopier. Transfer all notches, grain lines and pattern markings to the pattern.

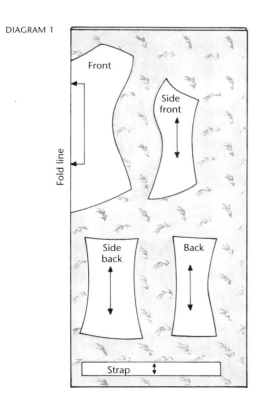

DIAGRAM 1

Front

Side front

Fold line

Side back

Back

Strap

- Fold the fabric in half with right sides together and selvages matching. Pin the pattern to the fabric, with the straight grain lines parallel to selvages (diagram 1). Pin and then cut the front of the bodice on the fold, cutting round the notches. Cut two of each of the remaining pattern pieces. Transfer all markings from the pattern to the fabric with dressmaker's chalk before unpinning the tissue paper.
- Using the same pattern pieces, pin and then cut the lining and interfacing for all sections of the bustier. Again, transfer all pattern markings to the fabric before removing the pattern.
- Press the fabric and lining sections of the bustier with a warm iron, ensuring that there are no creases.

Sewing

1 Pin the corresponding woven interfacing pieces to the wrong side of the fabric sections of the bustier. Stay stitch the two layers together around the edges using a straight stitch 13 mm (½ in) in from the cut edge. Press each section with a warm iron.

2 Working on the bustier front panel, right side of the fabric facing up, stitch a row of gathering stitches 13 mm (½ in) in from the raw edge between the bust notches (diagram 2).

3 With right sides of fabric together, pin each bustier side front to the side seams of the front panel. Match the notches at the bust and waist. Pull up the gathering stitching between the bust notches on the front panel so that the fabric is eased to fit between the notches on the side panels.

DIAGRAM 2

4 Stitch the seams together. Clip the curved seams, cutting small notches from the outer curves and snipping the seam allowance of the inner curves (diagram 3).

DIAGRAM 3

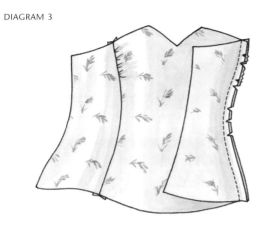

5 With the right sides of the fabric together, pin each bustier side back seam to the corresponding back seam, matching all the notches. Stitch the seams together. Clip the curved seams as before.

6 With the right sides of fabric together, pin then stitch the back to the front at the side seams. Clip the curved seams. Press all the seams open with a warm iron.

7 On the back opening edges press under 1.5 cm (⅝ in). Unzip the zipper and separate at the base.

8 With the right side of bustier back openings facing up, lap the pressed-under edge of the back seam over the zipper teeth. The fold of the back seams should be even with the zipper teeth. Pin the back seam allowance to the zipper and then baste the back seams of the bustier to each side of the zipper (diagram 4). Using a zipper foot, stitch the zipper, working approximately 6 mm (¼ in) away from the pressed fold. Remove the basting. See page 76 for zipper techniques.

DIAGRAM 4

9 Stitch the lining using the same method as for the bustier. Clip the seams. Press the seams closed and toward the back opening on either side of the bustier.

10 Cut the boning in lengths to fit all but the back opening seams. The boning should be cut from the inside seam at the top of the bustier to the waist measurement as marked on the original pattern. Pin and then stitch the boning to the wrong side of the lining close to the original seam stitching lines (diagram 5). Stitch through the centre of the boning to secure it to the lining seams.

DIAGRAM 5

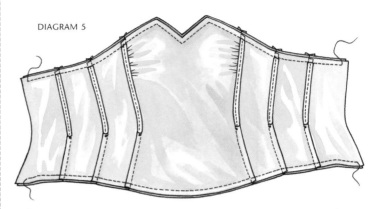

11 With right sides together, match the lining seams with the seams of the fabric bustier. Pin and then stitch the two layers together along the top and base of the bustier seams. Clip the point of the V in the centre front of the bustier (diagram 6).

DIAGRAM 6

12 Turn right side out through one of the back openings. Turn under and press the back seam allowance of the lining at the back opening. Slipstitch the lining to the edges of the zipper tapes (diagram 7).

DIAGRAM 7

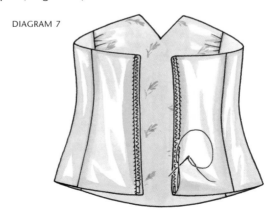

13 Stitch a hook and eye to the top of the back seam opening.

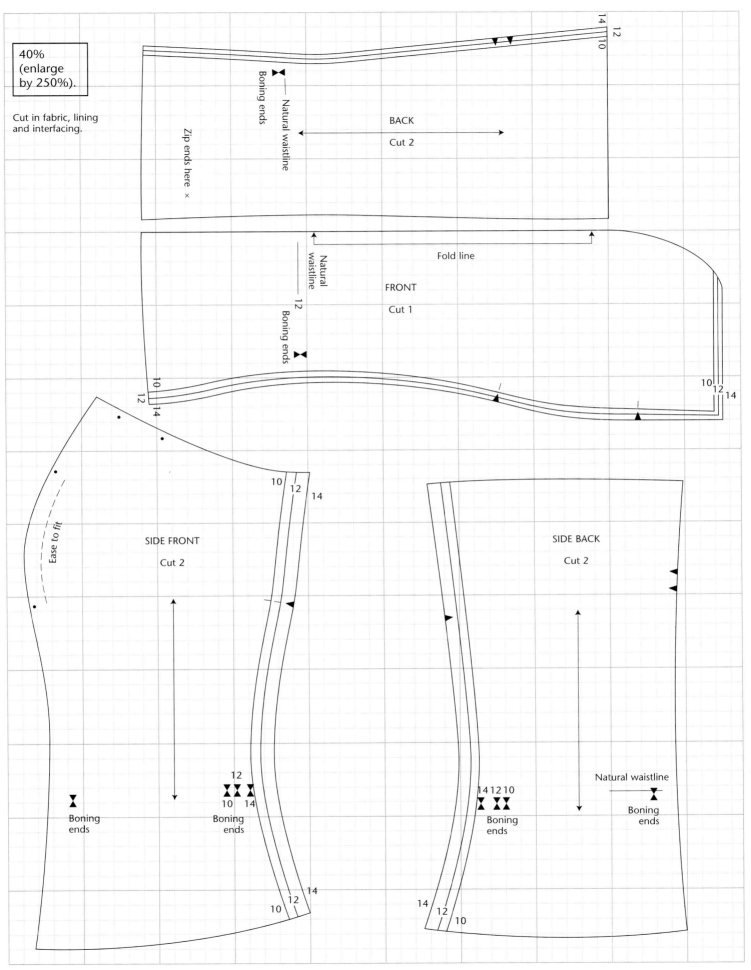

40%
(enlarge
by 250%).

Cut in fabric, lining
and interfacing.

Zip ends here ×

Boning ends

Natural waistline

BACK
Cut 2

14 12
10

Fold line

Natural waistline

FRONT
Cut 1

Boning ends

12

10 12 14

10
12 14

Ease to fit

SIDE FRONT
Cut 2

10 12 14

SIDE BACK
Cut 2

Natural waistline

Boning ends

12
10 14
Boning ends

14 12 10
Boning ends

Boning ends

14
12
10

14
12 10

Bustier with straps

This variation on the classic bustier has detachable straps, making it a really versatile garment. It can be dressed up for eveningwear, or worn with jeans or trousers for a glamorous daytime look.

Materials

1 m (1 yd) of 115 cm (45 in) wide silk, satin, brocade or dupion fabric
1 m (1 yd) of 115 cm (45 in) wide matching lining fabric
1 m (1 yd) of lightweight woven interfacing
2 reels of matching thread
Size 80 sewing machine needle
1.5 m (1½ yd) boning
25-cm (10-in) separating zipper
Hook and eye (optional)
Beads (optional)
Sharp fine crewel sewing needle (optional)

Cutting out

- Follow the cutting out instructions for the Classic bustier, page 128.
- Cut two straps 26 x 56 cm (10 x 22 in). Note: Cut on straight of grain parallel to the selvages. If they are cut on the fold, cut each strap 13 x 56 cm (5 x 22 in).

Sewing

1 Follow steps 1–8 of the Classic bustier, page 128.

2 Fold the straps in half with right sides together. Stitch a 6 mm (¼ in) seam down the cut edge. Turn the straps right side out and refold so the seam is in the centre. Tuck the raw ends inside and press flat.

3 Take a small pleat in the centre of the strap by folding it in half and pinning it 2.5 cm (1 in) in from the fold through all layers. Stitch vertically from the ends for approximately 7.5 cm (3 in). Open the fold so it lies flat against the body of the strap and press (diagram 1).

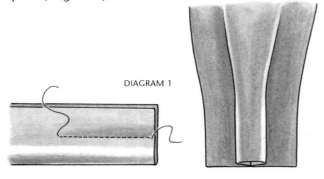

DIAGRAM 1

4 Pin the straps to the right side of the front seams of the bustier as indicated on the pattern. Attach the straps to the bustier matching one end of the strap with the markings on the bustier front seams. Stitch the straps to the seam line of the garment to hold them in place.

5 Stitch the lining using the same method as for the Classic bustier. Clip the seams. Press the seams closed and toward the back opening on either side of the bustier.

6 Cut the boning in lengths to fit all but the back opening seams. The boning should be cut from the inside seam at the top of the bustier to the waist measurement as marked on the original pattern. Pin and then stitch the boning to the wrong side of the lining close to the original seam stitching lines. Stitch through the centre of the boning to secure it to the lining seams (see diagram 5, page 130).

7 With right sides together, match the lining seams with the seams of the fabric bustier, sandwiching the straps at the front. Pin and then stitch the two layers together along the top, catching the straps in place on the front and leaving a gap to insert the straps at the back (diagram 2). Stitch the lining to the bustier at the base (making sure you do not inadvertently catch the straps in the stitching). Clip the point of the V in the centre front of the bustier.

DIAGRAM 2

8 Turn right side out through one of the back openings. Turn under and press the back seam allowance of the lining at the back opening. Slip stitch the lining to the edges of the zipper tapes.

9 Stitch a hook and eye to the top of the back seam opening.

10 Try the bustier on and adjust the length of the straps to fit, slipping them into the gap between the lining and the bustier at the back. Once satisfied, pin then top stitch in place. If desired, edge stitch all around the top, stitching a scant 3 mm (⅛ in) from the fabric edge.

Bodice decoration

1 Cut another thin strap 3 cm (1¼ in) wide by 1 m (3 ft) long. Fold in half lengthwise and stitch with a 6 mm (¼ in) seam allowance. Turn through and press. Tuck the raw edges under and slip stitch in place.

2 Stitch a gathering thread through the centre of the strap by machine stitching with the longest stitch possible. Tie one end of the gathering thread together in a knot. Gather up the trim so that it forms a frill long enough to fill the front edge of the bustier. Pin in place then hand stitch to the top edge of the bustier. Attach beads for a decorative finish.

Detachable straps

Make the straps detachable by machine stitching the ends once the raw edges are tucked under. Hand stitch press studs to the underside of the straps at either end. Hand stitch corresponding pieces of studs to the inside of the bustier at the desired position.

Tailored skirt

This classic-style lined skirt is easy to make and so versatile. Team it with a matching jacket or pretty blouse for the office, or a bustier and wrap for the evening.

Materials

1 m (1 yd) of 140 cm (54 in) wide linen
1 m (1 yd) of 150 cm (60 in) wide lining to match
2 reels of polyester thread
20-cm (8-in) concealed zipper
1 m (1 yd) of fusible waistband interfacing
Skirt hook and eye
Chalk or marker pen
Invisible/concealed zipper foot

Cutting out

- Copy the skirt pattern on page 137 onto pattern drafting paper, following the lines corresponding to your size. Alternatively, enlarge the pattern on a photocopier. Transfer all pattern markings to the paper.
- Fold the fabric in half lengthwise with right sides together and carefully pin the skirt pattern to main fabric, placing skirt front on fold, and making sure the straight of grain line is parallel to the selvage (diagram 1). If you need to lengthen at the hem edge remember to mark this on the fabric.
- Cut out the skirt from the linen, cutting around the notches. Prior to removing the pattern pieces, mark the darts on the wrong side of the fabric using either a chalk pencil or a tailor's tack (see Tailor's tacks, page 41).
- On a single layer of fabric, mark out the waistband – length of waist measurement plus 10 cm (4 in) by a depth of 10 cm (4 in).

DIAGRAM 1

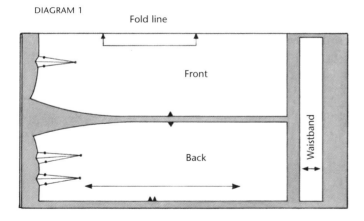

- Fold the lining fabric, right sides together, and cut out the skirt front and back as before. Again, mark the darts on the lining before removing the pattern pieces.

Sewing

1 Make the darts in the front of the skirt by bringing the two dots at the waist edge together and pinning. Machine stitch from the single dot on the fold of the dart towards the wide end of the dart (diagram 2). Secure the ends of stitching with a lock or fix stitch. Alternatively, tie the ends of the threads together.

DIAGRAM 2

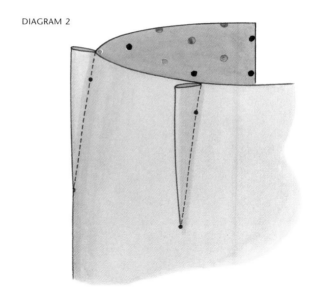

2 Press the darts, first pressing along the dart stitching from the wrong side and then preferably over a ham on the right side, pressing the fold toward the centre front. Make the darts in the skirt back in the same way. Press toward the centre back.

3 The concealed zipper is inserted prior to stitching the skirt pieces together. Working with the two back pieces, insert the zipper (see page 78).

4 Stitch the remainder of the centre back seam and then press the seam open. Neaten the edges of the centre back seam, using your preferred seam finish (overlock, zigzag stitch, turning raw edges under or pinking). Press from the right and wrong sides.

5 Join the skirt front to the skirt back at the side seams, right sides together. Press the seams open. Neaten as before and press again.

6 Make up the lining in exactly the same way as for the skirt, but instead of inserting a zipper at the centre, leave a 20-cm (8-in) opening in the seam.

7 Place the skirt and the lining together, wrong side to wrong side, matching the side seams and the centre back at the waist. Baste together at the waist (diagram 3).

DIAGRAM 3

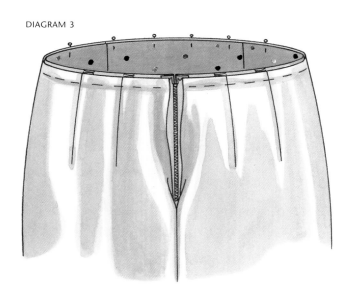

8 Fuse the waistband interfacing onto the wrong side of the waistband.

9 Pin the waistband to the upper edge of the skirt, right sides together, so that at one end the band overlaps by 1.5 cm (⅝ in) and at the other end it overlaps by 4 cm (1½ in). Trim off any excess. Machine stitch in place from side edge to side edge (diagram 4).

DIAGRAM 4

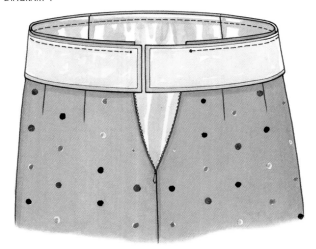

10 Layer this seam by trimming the skirt side of the seam down to half its width. Press the seam up into the waistband.

11 Neaten the edge of the waistband that is not attached to the skirt using the same technique used to neaten the side seams.

12 Make the ends of the waistband as follows. With the centre back right side out, fold the waistband right sides together and stitch the end from top to bottom in line with the centre back seam. On the right-hand end of the waistband, stitch a line continuing from the waist seam on the skirt for 2.5 cm (1 in) and then pivot and stitch at right angles to this to seal the end of the waistband (diagram 5).

DIAGRAM 5

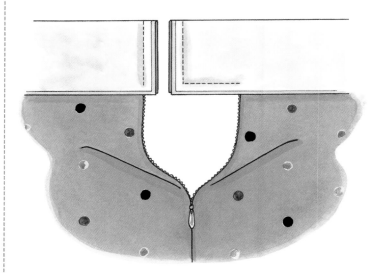

13 Trim the ends of the waistband seams. Turn to the right side so the waist raw edges are encased. Press.

14 To finish the waistband, pin securely in place, placing the pins at 90 degrees to the waist seam. Stitch in the ditch on the right side of the skirt or hand stitch the inside of the waistband to the lining.

15 Sew a skirt hook and eye onto the ends of the waistband. The right-hand side of the waistband goes under the left-hand side.

16 Neaten the raw edge of the skirt, using the same technique used on the side seams. Turn up the skirt hem by 5 cm (2 in) and baste. Finish the hem with blind hem stitch by hand or machine.

17 Remove the basting stitches and steam the hem carefully, avoiding pressing the edge too firmly (hems on tailored skirts should not be pressed into a sharp crease).

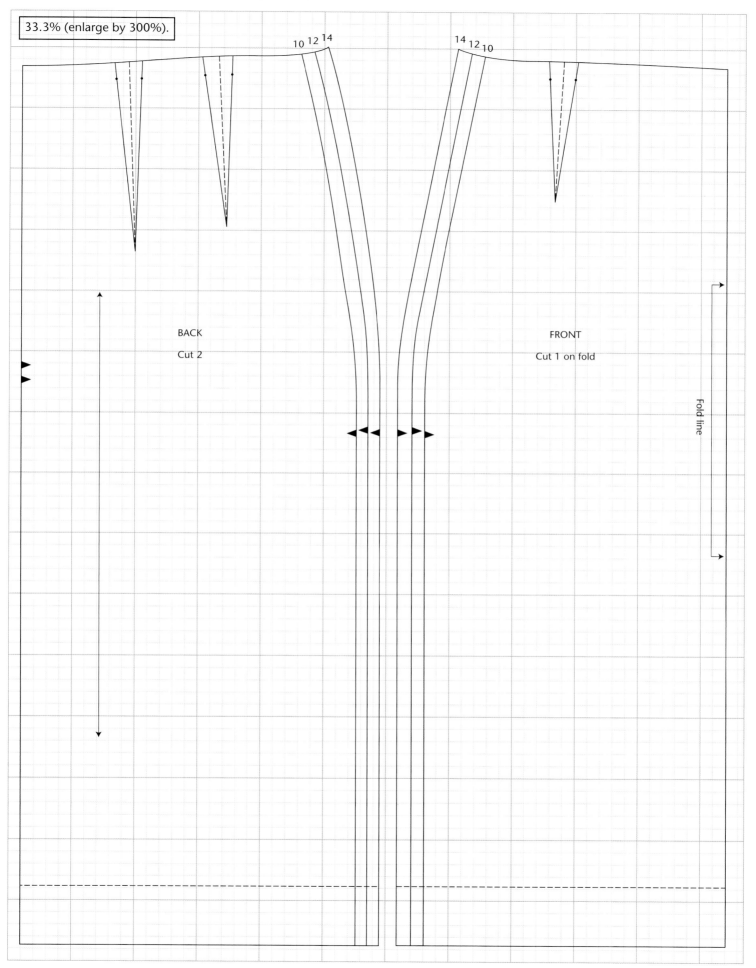

33.3% (enlarge by 300%).

10 12 14

14 12 10

BACK

Cut 2

FRONT

Cut 1 on fold

Fold line

Bias-cut skirt with frill

A tailored straight skirt can be easily adapted to a new style by cutting on the bias and adding a flippant frill.

Materials

140 cm (1½ yd) of 150 cm (60 in) wide linen or cotton fabric
140 cm (1½ yd) of 150 cm (60 in) wide lining to match
2 reels of polyester sewing thread
20-cm (8-in)) concealed zipper
90 cm (1 yd) fusible waistband interfacing
Skirt hook and eye

Preparation

- Copy the Tailored skirt pattern on page 137 onto pattern drafting paper, marking the centre back seam on the back as 'fold' so that there is only one back piece and only one front piece (the zipper will be inserted in the side seam).
- Remove 4 cm (1½ in) from the hem edge of both pattern pieces.
- Cut the waistband as for the Tailored skirt.

DIAGRAM 1

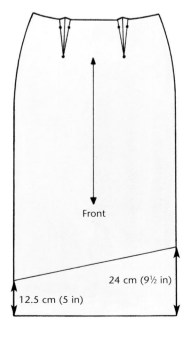
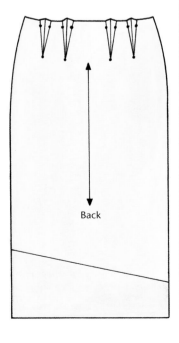

Front

Back

24 cm (9½ in)

12.5 cm (5 in)

Marking out the frill section

1 Working from the right-hand hem edge of the skirt front, measure up the side seam 24 cm (9½ in) and make a mark with a pencil.

2 Working from the left-hand hem edge of the skirt front, measure up the side seam 12.5 cm (5 in) and make a mark with a pencil. Use a ruler to join these two marks together, drawing a diagonal line across the paper.

3 This time, working on the left-hand hem edge of the skirt back, measure up the side seam 24 cm (9½ in) and mark with a pencil. On the right-hand edge, measure up the side seam 12.5 cm (5 in) and mark. Again join the marks using a ruler to draw a diagonal line (diagram 1).

4 Place the right side of the skirt back pattern on top of the right side skirt front pattern and check that the diagonal lines drawn start and finish in the same place on the side seams. If they are not the same, adjust them.

5 Label the skirt section above the line 'skirt front' or 'skirt back' and on both mark 'cut 1'. Draw in a grain line down the centre front or centre back of each piece, ensuring the grain line continues onto the lower sections of the skirt. Label the lower skirt sections 'skirt front/back frill' and 'cut 1'. Cut along the diagonal line.

6 Take the lower skirt frill sections and divide them into eight pieces each. Draw the lines on with a ruler and pencil from the hem edge to the top edge. Cut along the pencil lines to within 3 mm (⅛ in) of the top edge.

7 Place these cut sections on to a larger piece of pattern paper. Keeping the section in the centre on the straight of the grain, spread the remainder out evenly so there is a gap of

DIAGRAM 2

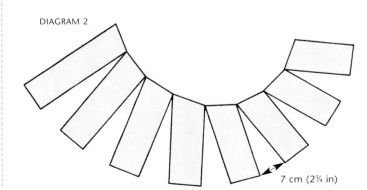

7 cm (2¾ in)

approximately 7 cm (2¾ in) between each cut line. Secure to the new piece of pattern paper. Make sure that the back and front sections are spread evenly (diagram 2).

8 Add a seam allowance of 1.5 cm (⅝ in) to the top edge of the frill sections. Cut out the spread frill piece. Add a seam allowance to the lower diagonal edge of the skirt sections.

9 Working on a single layer of fabric, right side uppermost, lay the pattern pieces on the fabric, also right side up, ensuring the straight of grain is parallel with the selvages (diagram 3). Mark the darts using a chalk pencil or tailor's tacks. Cut out, cutting around the notches.

10 Use the same pattern pieces to cut out the lining. Again mark the darts in position.

Helpful hint: The more you can spread out the frill sections, the more fullness you will have at the lower edge of the skirt.

Sewing

1 Make the darts in the skirt front and back as for the Tailored skirt and press.

2 With right sides together, join the front skirt frill to the skirt front and the back skirt frill to the skirt back. Press open the seams and neaten the seams with overlock or zigzag stitch.

3 Insert a concealed zipper into the left-hand side seam (see page 78).

4 Complete the left-hand side seam and stitch the right-hand side seam, matching the points where the frill seams meet. Press the seams open and neaten.

5 Repeat for the lining, leaving a gap in the lining where the zipper is in the skirt. Baste the lining and the skirt together at the waist seam, wrong sides together.

6 Attach the waistband as for the Tailored skirt, page 136.

7 Neaten the hem edge on the skirt with overlock or zigzag stitch. Turn up the hem edge on the skirt 1 cm (⅜ in) and baste in place. Press gently to eliminate any fullness and then machine stitch in place with a straight stitch.

8 Make a double hem in the lining by turning up 1 cm (⅜ in) twice, so the neatened raw edge meets the first fold. Machine stitch in place. Press.

DIAGRAM 3

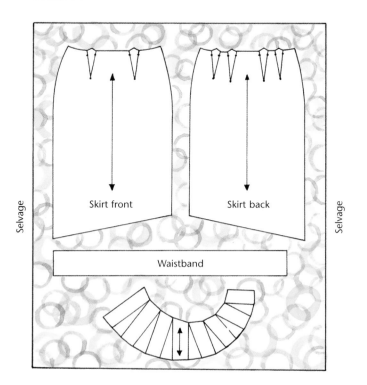

Evening skirt

Another variation on the tailored skirt, this elegant evening version is full length and has a godet added to the back seam.

Materials

2 m (2¼ yd) of 150 cm (60 in) wide satin, duchess silk or other evening fabric
2 m (2¼ yd) of 150 cm (60 in) wide lining to match
2–3 reels polyester thread
20-cm (8-in) concealed zipper
Skirt hook and eye

Cutting out

1 Copy the Tailored skirt pattern on page 137 onto pattern drafting paper, lengthening it at the hem edge by 43 cm (17 in). Alternatively, enlarge the pattern on a photocopier. Transer all pattern markings to the paper.

2 At the centre back hem edge of the pattern measure in by 2.5 cm (1 in) and make a mark (diagram 1). Make another mark on the centre back seam approximately 41 cm (16 in) below the waist.

3 Draw a line between these two marks and then remove this section from the pattern. Add a seam allowance of 1.5 cm (⅝ in) back on along this edge. Measure the diagonal length of the edge that you have just removed and make a note of the measurement, now called A.

4 The godet is shaped like the section of a circle. If you wish the godet to drape on the floor behind the skirt you will need to establish the amount of fabric that is to puddle on the floor. To do this, measure from the hem edge along the floor and make a note of this number as well and mark it B.

5 Draw out this segment on a large piece of pattern paper (diagram 2). The angle at the top of the segment determines the amount of fullness. Choose between a 30-degree angle up to a 90-degree angle or more. The one in the photograph had a 60-degree angle. The length of the diagonal sides is measurement A. The depth of the curved puddle piece that will drape on the floor is measurement B. Add a seam allowance to all edges.

DIAGRAM 1

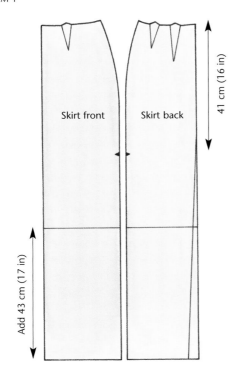

DIAGRAM 2

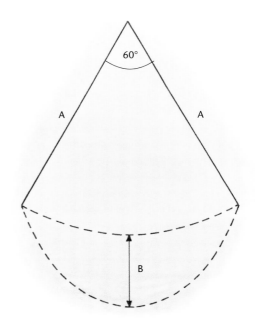

6 Fold the fabric in half, right sides together and position the skirt front and back as shown in diagram 3, placing the front on the fold and the back so that the straight of grain is parallel to the selvages. Cut out, cutting around the notches. Open out the fabric and with the fabric right side up, cut the godet and waistband from a single layer, again with the straight of grain parallel to the selvages.

DIAGRAM 3

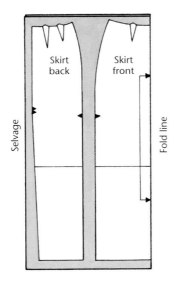

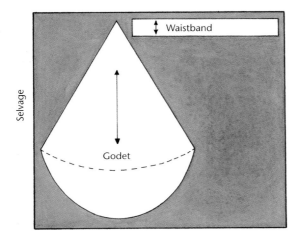

7 Cut lining fabric from the same pattern pieces in the same way.

Sewing

1 Make up the darts and press as for the Tailored skirt.

2 Neaten the seam edges of the centre back seam. Neaten the long edges of the godet section (not the lower curved edge).

3 Insert a concealed zipper at the centre back (see page 78) and then complete the centre back seam to the point where the godet is to be inserted.

4 Pin and stitch one side of the godet in place. Pin and stitch the other side of the godet in place. Make sure all the stitching lines meet at the top (diagram 4).

DIAGRAM 4

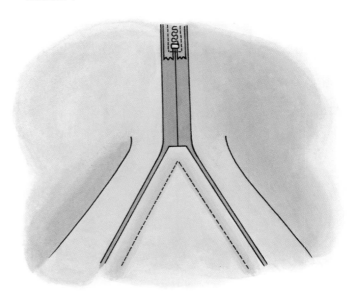

5 Press the seams to one side. Join the front to the back at the side seams, matching the notches. Stitch the seam. Neaten and press.

6 Make up the lining to match. Baste the lining and skirt together at the waist and attach the waistband as for the Tailored skirt.

7 Wearing appropriate shoes, check the skirt for length. The front of a long skirt should just touch the top of the shoe. Mark the hem with chalk.

8 Neaten the raw hem edge of the skirt and turn up to the marked position and blind hem stitch in place by hand.

Helpful hint: *A hem of approximately 3.5 cm (1½ in) is the ideal depth.*

9 Make a double hem in the lining by turning up 2.5 cm (1 in) twice so the neatened raw edge meets the first fold. Machine stitch in place.

Long cardigan coat

This classic garment can be made in day or evening fabrics. This one has a bias trim rather than facings making it a simple project, perfect for novice sewers. The classic design of the coat has been embellished with satin bias trim and glass beads to create an understated elegant evening look.

Materials

3 m (3¼ yd) of 115 cm (45 in) wide lightweight wool, crêpe, polyester, lace or chiffon

3 m (3¼ yd) of 2 cm (¾ in) wide satin bias trim

2 reels of polyester sewing thread

Dressmaker's chalk

Overlocker (optional)

Sharp fine crewel sewing needle (optional)

Collection of beads (optional)

Hook and eye (optional)

Cutting out

- Copy the pattern on page 147 onto pattern drafting paper, following the lines corresponding to your size. Alternatively, enlarge the pattern on a photocopier. Transfer all pattern markings to the paper.
- Fold the fabric in half lengthwise and lay out the pattern as shown in diagram 1, placing the back on the fold and the front and sleeves with the straight of grain line parallel with the selvages. Cut out, cutting round the notches. Transfer all markings from the pattern to the fabric with dressmaker's chalk before removing the pattern.

Sewing

1 Overlock or zigzag the edges of the shoulder, front and back coat side seams and the front and back seams of the sleeves.

2 With right sides together, pin and stitch the fronts to the back at the shoulder seams. Press the seams open and flat.

3 Pin and stitch the side seams of the front and back of the coat together. This may be done with a 4-thread overlocker or sewing machine set on straight stitch.

4 With right sides together, pin and stitch the sleeve seams from the armhole down to the wrist. Press the seam open and flat.

5 To ease the top of the sleeve, use a long machine stitch to sew a row of stitches just inside the seam line between the easing dots marked on the pattern. Stitch a second row of stitching 6 mm (¼ in) inside the seam line (diagram 2).

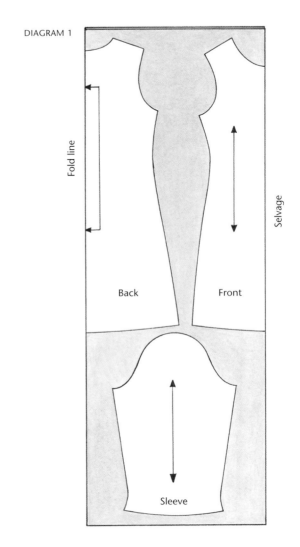

DIAGRAM 1

Fold line

Selvage

Back

Front

Sleeve

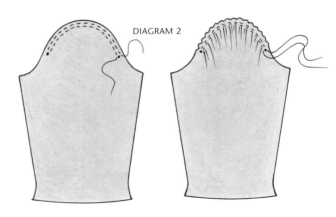

DIAGRAM 2

6 Pull up the ease stitches to create a soft, gathered head on the sleeves. Turn the sleeves right sides out.

7 To fit the sleeve into the armhole of the coat, hold the garment wrong side out with the armhole facing toward you. With right sides together, pin the sleeve into the armhole with the centre small dot on the head of the sleeve matching the shoulder seam (diagram 3). Carefully match the underarm seam of the sleeve with the side seams of the coat. Match the front and back notches.

DIAGRAM 3

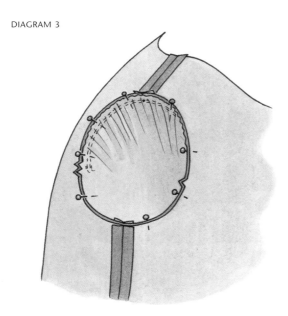

8 Distribute the gathers at the top of the sleeve evenly between the front and back dots marked on both the sleeve and coat. Baste then stitch the sleeves into place. Overlock or zigzag the raw edges of the seams together. Clip the curves of the underarm toward the stitching.

9 Turn up the hem of the sleeve and machine stitch in place. For a decorative finish stitch a length of bias trim over the hemmed sleeve stitching.

10 To finish the neckline of the coat, open one folded edge of the bias trim, pin and then stitch to the wrong side of the coat, stitching along the bias trim fold line. Trim off the excess fabric from the seam allowance, level with the raw edge of the bias trim. Fold the bias trim to the front of the garment covering the raw edges of the seam. Pin then stitch as close to the folded edge of the bias tape as possible, securing the bias trim to the neck edge of the coat (diagram 4).

DIAGRAM 4

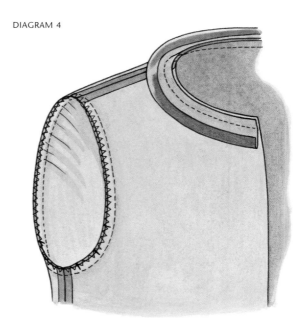

11 Pin a length of bias trim to the wrong side of the centre front seams, extending it 2 cm (¾ in) beyond the bound neck edge. Fold over the bias extension, flush with the finished neck seam. Baste the fold in place and then continue to attach the bias trim as in step 10.

12 To finish the coat attach bias trim to the raw edge of the hem line as in step 11 above and add a hook and eye at the neckline.

> ### Finishing touches
> Shoulder pads may be attached to the inside shoulder seams if desired. For a decorative effect at the neckline, hand stitch beads and trims.

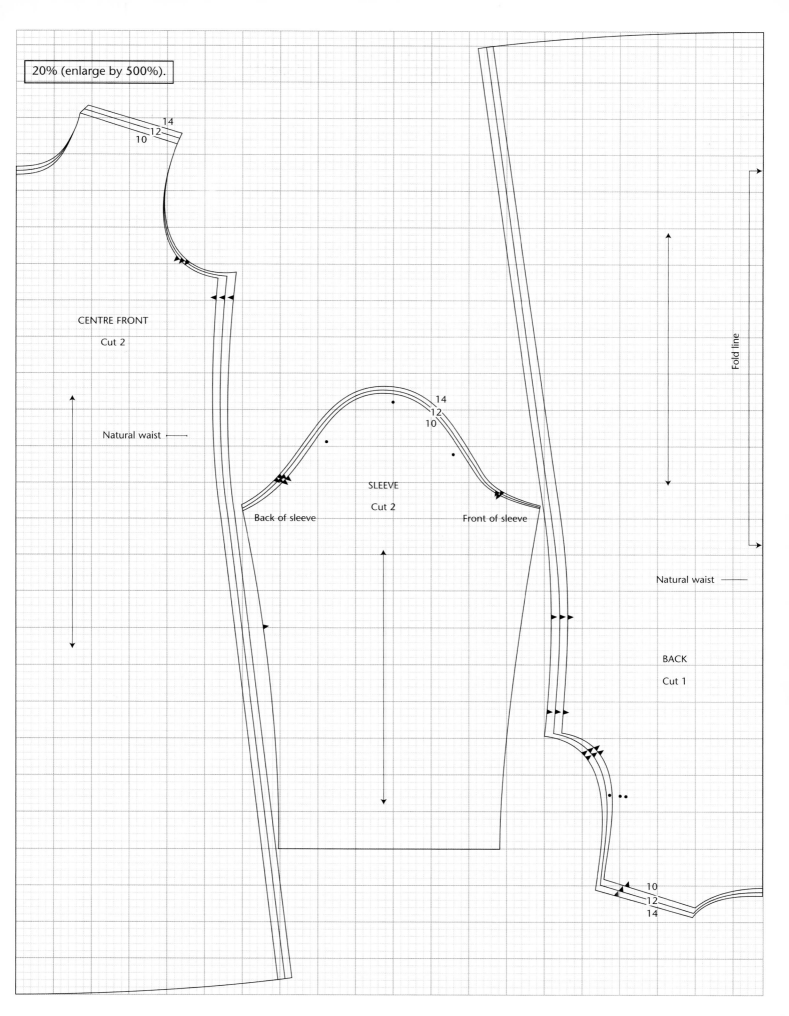

20% (enlarge by 500%).

CENTRE FRONT

Cut 2

Natural waist

14
12
10

SLEEVE

Cut 2

Back of sleeve   Front of sleeve

14
12
10

Fold line

Natural waist

BACK

Cut 1

10
12
14

Simple summer dress

Make this classically shaped dress in a soft draping print for summer or luxury silks for evenings.

Materials

160 cm (2 yd) of 150 cm (60 in) wide medium-weight viscose crêpe
OR 220 cm (2½ yd) of 115 cm (45 in) wide
25 cm (¼ yd) of very lightweight fusible interfacing
40-cm (16-in) lightweight zipper
1 small hook and eye/bar
2 reels polyester thread
Chalk marker
Rouleau turner (optional)

Cutting out

- Copy the pattern on page 151 onto pattern drafting paper, following the lines corresponding to your size and the cutting lines for the dress. Alternatively, enlarge the pattern on a photocopier. Transfer all pattern markings to the paper.
- Fold the fabric in half lengthwise with right sides together and lay out the pattern as shown in diagram 1, with the front

on the fold and the back positioned so the straight of grain line is parallel with the selvages. Cut out, cutting around the notches. Position the front facing to the fold and cut one. Cut two back facings and two straps.
- Using the same pattern pieces, cut front and back facings in fusible interfacing.
- Transfer all notches, darts and zipper placement to the wrong side of the fabric with a chalk marker.

Sewing

1 Make the straps by folding the fabric in half lengthwise with the right sides together. Machine stitch 6 mm (¼ in) from the folded edge. Without trimming the seam allowance, turn through with a rouleau turner. Alternatively, snip a small hole close to one end and insert one end of a hair grip to pull the end through. Set aside until needed later (diagram 2).

DIAGRAM 2

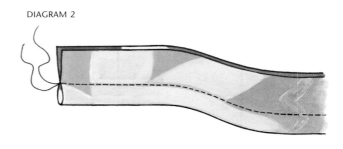

Helpful hint: Leaving the seam allowance untrimmed helps to fill out the finished strap giving it a more rounded appearance.

2 Sew the darts on the front and back pieces, stitching from the tapered point to the widest part on the bust dart and from point to point on the front and back waist darts. Press lightly with the bust darts facing downward and the waist darts to the centre. Use a pressing cloth if necessary (see Helpful hints, page 150).

3 Pin the back sections, right sides together, notches matching. Insert a zipper into the centre back using your preferred method (see page 76). Machine stitch the rest of the centre back seam, press the seam allowances open and neaten the raw edges.

DIAGRAM 1

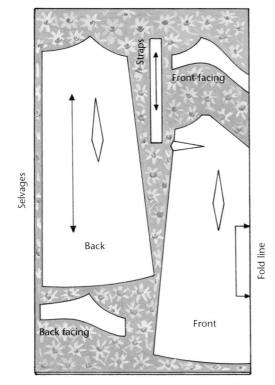

4 With right sides together, place the front and the back together with the side seams matching (diagram 3). Pin and machine stitch. Neaten the seams with your preferred method and press lightly.

DIAGRAM 3

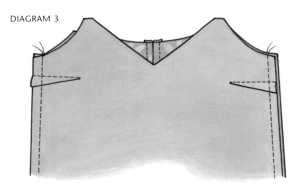

5 Trim 1.5 cm (⅝ in) from the interfacing pieces and then fuse them onto the wrong side of the front and back facings. Allow to cool completely before handling again.

6 Pin and stitch the front to the back facings at the side seams. Trim the seam allowance. Neaten the lower edge of the facing with overlock or zigzag stitch or by turning the raw edge to the wrong side and stitching in place.

7 Place the facing to the top edge of the dress with right sides together. Pin the straps in position at the front only, sandwiching the straps between the facing and the dress. Making sure the side seams match, machine stitch along the top edge, securing the straps at the front and leaving a gap in the stitching at the two back strap positions. These will be sewn after fitting has taken place (diagram 4).

DIAGRAM 4

8 Sew over the stitching at the centre front approximately 2.5 cm (1 in) either side of the centre point to reinforce the seam. Snip into this so that when turned through, a good shape is achieved. Lightly press the facing seam open and trim.

Facing applied to the top edge of the dress.

Helpful hint: Pressing an enclosed seam open helps it to lie flat when turned through.

9 Try the dress on and pin the straps in place to determine their correct length. Insert the straps through the small gaps left at the back. Turn through and machine stitch securely in place on the inside (diagram 5).

DIAGRAM 5

10 Press lightly. Edge stitch around the top edge if desired (this helps to keep the facing inside).

11 Turn up a narrow double hem by turning under 1 cm (⅜ in) twice so the raw edge meets the first fold. Machine stitch in place.

Helpful hints • *Pre-shrink the entire length of fabric before starting to cut out by lightly pressing with a steam iron. Leave to dry and cool before cutting out as normal*
• *Use a piece of 100% silk organza as a pressing cloth. It will withstand the heat of the iron and the garment being pressed can be seen through the organza.*

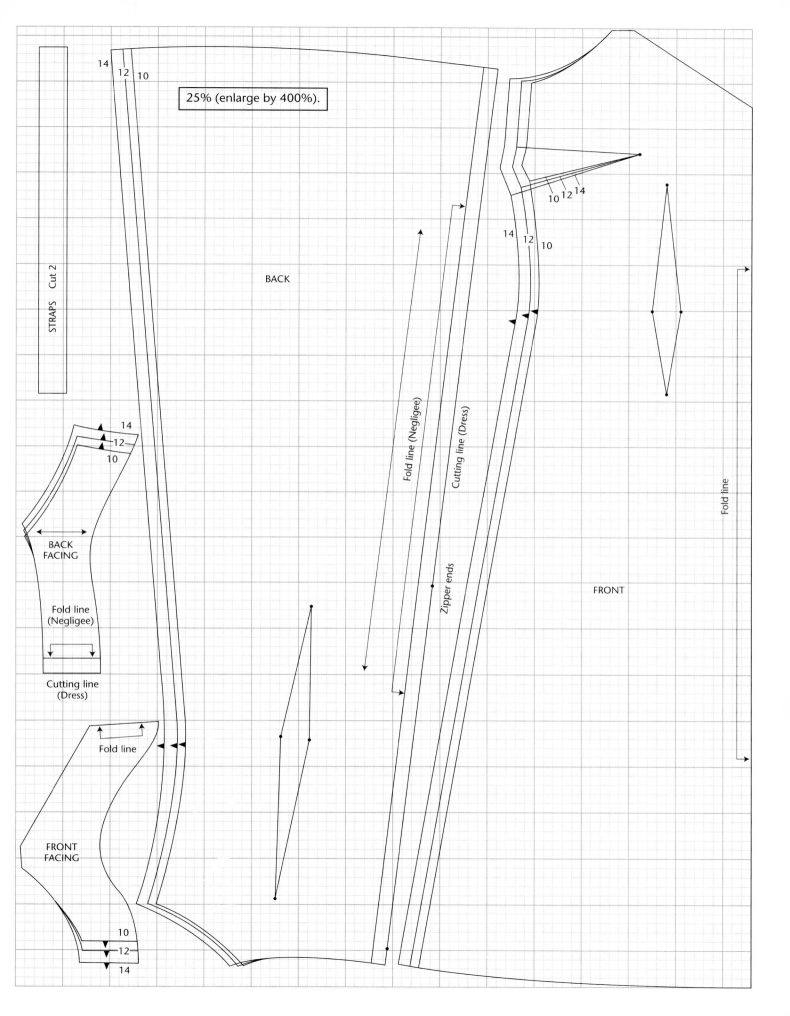

25% (enlarge by 400%).

STRAPS   Cut 2

14
12 10

BACK

14
12
10

BACK
FACING

Fold line
(Negligee)

Cutting line
(Dress)

Fold line (Negligee)

Cutting line (Dress)

Zipper ends

10 12 14

14
12 10

FRONT

Fold line

Fold line

FRONT
FACING

10
12
14

Negligée

Made from the same basic pattern as the dress, the negligée is cut on the cross and has no back seam or centre back zipper. It is therefore comfortable to wear and has a delightful elegant drape.

Materials

220 cm (2½ yd) of 150 cm (60 in) wide silk or polyester satin
3 m (3¼ yd) edging lace
1 reel of polyester thread
Rouleau turner
Walking foot (optional)

Cutting out

- Copy the pattern on page 151 for the negligée on to pattern drafting paper, using the centre back position for the negligée rather than the dress line. Alternatively, enlarge the pattern on a photocopier. Transfer all pattern markings to the paper. In order to get one front and one back without centre seams it is necessary to mirror the front piece to get a left and right side, with the centre front seam at the centre. Repeat for the back.
- With the fabric open as a single layer, place the pattern pieces on the fabric as shown in diagram 1. Note the centre front and centre back are now at a 45-degree angle to the selvage and not parallel to it. Cut out, cutting around the notches.
- Cut out the straps and the facings with the straight of grain line parallel to the selvages. Note: interfacings are not used on the negligée to avoid unnecessary bulk.
- Transfer the pattern markings for the bust darts only. The waist darts (front and back) will not be used for the negligée.

Sewing

1 Make straps for the negligée by folding lengthwise with right sides together. Machine stitch 6 mm (¼ in) from the raw edges. Turn through with a rouleau turner or hair grip.

2 Edge stitch along both long edges to create a flat and narrow strap approximately 1 cm (⅜ in) wide. Make sure you edge stitch the seam edge first, tucking the seam slightly to the wrong side. Follow by machining the opposite edge, stitching both in the same direction. This will give a neater finish. Set these aside until required (diagram 2).

3 Pin and sew the bust darts on the front of the negligée. Lightly press downward when completed, using a pressing cloth if necessary.

DIAGRAM 1

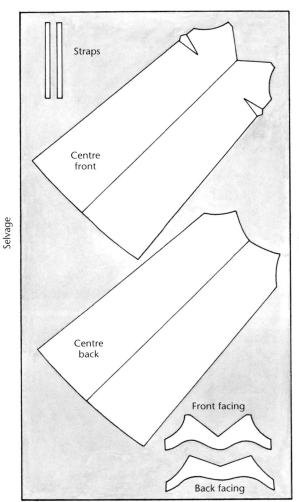

DIAGRAM 2

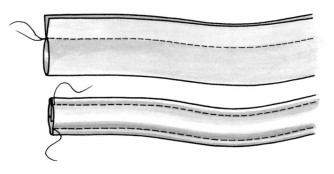

4 Join the side seams together with French seams (with wrong sides together, match notches and stitch 6 mm (¼ in) from the edge). Trim the seam allowance to 3 mm (⅛ in) and press. Turn through so the right sides are together and stitch the seam again, taking a 1 cm (⅜ in) seam allowance and encasing the raw edges as you sew. Press again.

Helpful hint: To avoid the bias seam from rippling, use a walking foot on your sewing machine.

5 Sew together the front and back facings with right sides together. Neaten the lower edge with overcast or zigzag stitch.

6 Pin the facing to the top edge of the negligée with right sides together. Pin the straps in position at the front only. Making sure the side seams match, machine stitch along the top edge, securing the straps at the front and leaving a gap in the stitching at the two back strap positions. These will be sewn after fitting has taken place.

7 Sew over the stitching at the centre front approximately 2.5 cm (1 in) either side of the centre point to reinforce the seam. Snip into this so that when turned through, a good shape is achieved (diagram 3).

DIAGRAM 3

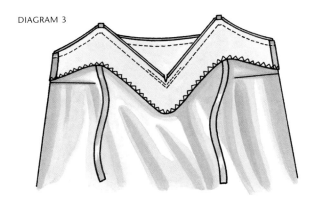

8 Lightly press the facing seam open and trim. (Pressing an enclosed seam open helps it to lie flat when turned through.)

9 Try the negligée on and pin the straps in place to determine their correct length. Insert through the small gaps left for the straps at the back. Turn through and securely machine stitch in place on the inside. Press lightly. Edge stitch along the top edge if desired.

Helpful hint: To stitch close to the edge, move the needle position to the far right and use the inner edge of the presser foot as a stitching guide.

10 Neaten the raw hem edge of the negligée, then turn a narrow hem and machine stitch in place (diagram 4). Use a walking foot to prevent rippling. Alternatively, make a rippling lettuce hem by pulling gently on the hem edge as it is stitched which will stretch the fabric slightly. Once relaxed it ripples into little waves.

DIAGRAM 4

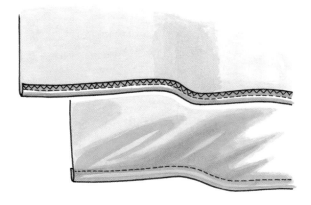

11 Finish the hem and top edges with lace attached by hand or by using the sewing machine.

Kimono-style dressing gown

Enjoy a relaxing night in wearing this comfortable robe. Based on the Japanese kimono style, it is made up of a combination of rectangles.

Materials

3–4 m (3–4 yd) of 115 cm (45 in) wide silk, polyester or towelling *

2 m (2¼ yd) of 50 cm (20 in) lightweight fusible interfacing

Marking pen/chalk marker and ruler

*The amount of fabric will depend on the length or height – it needs to be at least double height from the shoulders.

Cutting out

- Determine the size of the rectangles for the front and back by measuring as follows (diagram 1):
  - Length: shoulder to ankle – add 5 cm (2 in) for hems.
  - Width: across back of body at widest part (bust/chest or hip) from side to side. Add 3 cm (1½ in) for seam allowances.
  - Bands: length plus 15 cm (6 in)
- For the fronts, halve the width measurement and add 14 cm (5½ in) for the wrap-over. Fold the fabric in half lengthwise and cut two rectangles to the length/width calculated for the wrap fronts.
- Open out the fabric, and following the layout shown in diagram 2, cut another rectangle to the length and full width measurement for back.
  - Cut two sleeves 29 x 66 cm (11½ x 26 in)
  - Cut two bands, length determined earlier x 14 cm (5½ in) wide
  - Cut two pocket pieces 16 x 25 cm (6¼ x 10 in)
  - Cut two belt loops 3 x 20 cm (1½ x 8 in)
  - Cut two belt pieces 14 x 100 cm (5½ x 40 in)
- Cut fusible interfacing for the band and belt – each strip the length x 12 cm (5 in) wide.

DIAGRAM 1

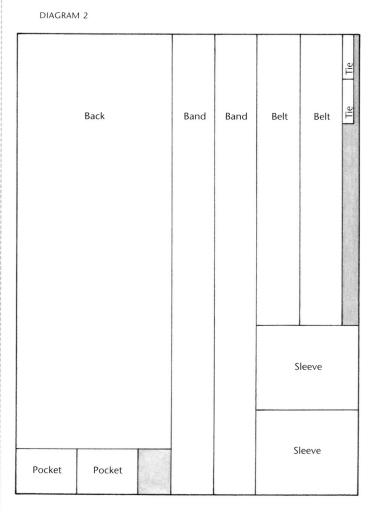

DIAGRAM 2

Back | Band | Band | Belt | Belt | Tie | Tie

Sleeve

Sleeve

Pocket | Pocket

Fold line

Front

Cut 2

Sewing

1 Centre the strips of interfacing on the wrong side of the band and belt pieces and fuse in place (diagram 3).

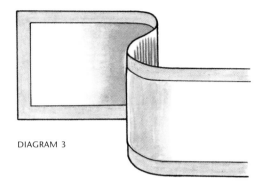

DIAGRAM 3

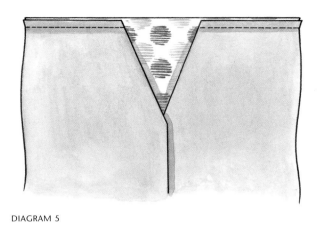

DIAGRAM 5

2 With right sides together, join the band pieces together at one short end to make a long strip. Press and leave to one side.

3 Stitch the short ends of the belt pieces together to make one long strip. Fold in half lengthwise, right sides together, and sew across the ends and up the long side, leaving a turning gap of 30 cm (12 in) in the middle of the strip. Trim the seam allowances and turn through. Press and slipstitch the opening closed. Set to one side.

4 Take one belt loop strip, fold lengthwise with right sides together and stitch, taking a 6 mm (¼ in) seam allowance. Turn through and press. Fold in half to make a loop, pin in place. Repeat for other loop. Set to one side.

5 With one front section on a flat surface wrong side up, fold back the right edge 22 cm (8½ in), tapering to nothing, 43 cm (17 in) down the side. This creates the shaping for the front. Finger press in place, then cut off the long triangular shape, leaving a 1.5 cm (⅝ in) seam allowance. Open out the fold, then place the cut piece, right sides together, over the remaining front. Cut a mirror image piece from second front (diagram 4).

7 Fold the sleeves in half lengthwise and finger press at the fold to find the centre. Open out and, with the robe front and back opened out, match the centre of the sleeve to the shoulder seam, pinning right sides together. Machine stitch together, starting and finishing 1.5 cm (⅝ in) from either end (diagram 6).

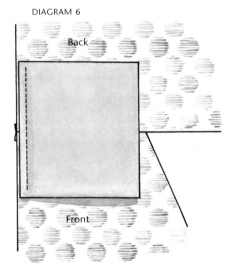

DIAGRAM 6

Back

Front

8 With right sides together, pin the side seams from the sleeve edge to the hem of the robe. At approximate waist level, pin one tie within the seam allowance so the loop is sandwiched between the fabric layers. Stitch from the sleeve edge to the hem of the garment, catching the loop ends in place (diagram 7). Clip the seam allowances at the curves and neaten with zigzag or overcast stitch. Press.

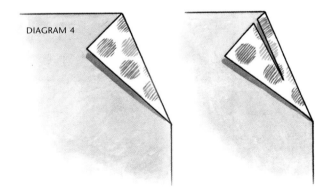

DIAGRAM 4

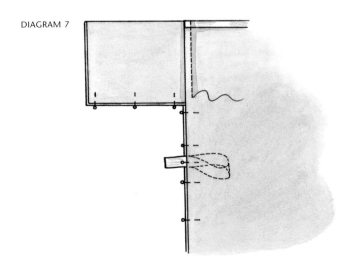

DIAGRAM 7

6 Place the shoulder seams right sides together and stitch the fronts to the back along the top, taking a 1.5 cm (⅝ in) seam allowance (diagram 5). There should be approximately 18 cm (7 in) of back free at the centre (back neck). Press.

9 Place the pocket sections, right sides together, and stitch all around, taking a 6 mm (¼ in) seam allowance and leaving a turning gap in one short end for turning. Press, clip the seams and cut off the corners. Turn through and press again. Slip stitch the opening closed. Measure down 2.5 cm (1 in) from the opposite short end and top stitch from side to side.

Helpful hint: Strengthen the top of the pocket opening by stitching a small triangle (see below).

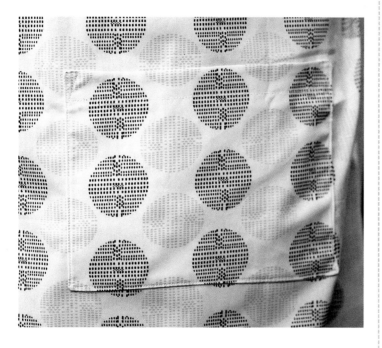

10 Try on the robe and mark the pocket position with a marking pen or chalk pencil, making sure the top is horizontal. Pin the pocket in place and machine stitch the sides and bottom a scant 3 mm (⅛ in) from the pocket edges.

11 With right sides together, fold the band in half lengthwise. At either end, 5 cm (2 in) from the end, stitch from the fold to within 1.5 cm (⅝ in) of the edge to hem the band (diagram 8). Then turn one long edge under 1.5 cm (⅝ in) and press.

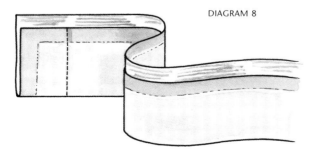

DIAGRAM 8

12 Open out the band and then, starting at the seam midway along the band, pin the raw edge of the band to the neck edge, right sides together, with the seam at the centre of the neck back. Pin down the fronts, pivoting and clipping the seam allowance at the shoulders and matching the side edges with the raw edge on the band (diagram 9). Machine stitch the band in place. Clip and grade the seam allowances.

DIAGRAM 9

13 Refold the band to encase the raw edges of the seam and pin the folded band edge so it just covers the seam line on the inside. Either slip stitch in place on the inside, or top stitch from the right side, stitching in the ditch (see page 46), catching the underside in place (diagram 10).

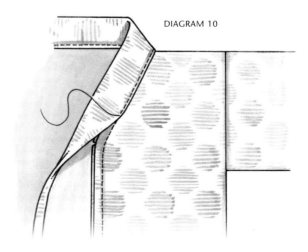

DIAGRAM 10

14 At the hem edge, turn up the robe hem along the same fold line as the band, tucking the raw edge under again to encase. Top stitch or blind hem stitch by hand.

15 Finish the sleeve edges by turning the hem allowance under 5 cm (2 in), tucking the raw edge under to encase and top stitching in place.

Suppliers and Useful Addresses

UNITED KINGDOM

Most large department stores carry a good range of fabrics, threads and accessories. For specific materials or information, contact details of specialist suppliers are also given.

Crowson and Monkwell Fabrics
Crowson House
Bellbrook Park
Uckfield
East Sussex TN22 1QZ
Tel: 01825 761055
Fax: 01825 764517
Email:
sales@crowsonfabrics.com
Offers a wide range of fabrics for dressmaking

Fabrics for Perfect Occasions
Woodhead Road
Bradford
West Yorkshire
BD7 1PB
Tel: 01274 414887
Fax: 01274 308515
Email: bryan@fabricsforperfect
    occasions.co.uk
Offers a wide range of fabrics for dressmaking

Groves & Banks
Drakes Drive Industrial Estate
Long Credon
Aylesbury
Bucks
HP18 9BA
Tel: 01844 258080
Fax: 01844 258058
Email: sales@groves-banks.com
www.groves-banks.com
Major distributor of sewing accessories and needlecrafts. Contact for details of UK stockists

Perival Gütermann
Bullsbrook Road
Hayes
Middlesex UB4 OJR
www.gütermann.com
Producer of quality sewing threads

Janome Sewing Machines
Janome Centre
Southside
Cheshire SK6 2SP
Tel: 0161 666 6011
Fax: 0161 406 6401
www.janome.co.uk
Largest manufacturer of domestic sewing machines. Useful website with information and online store

John Kaldor Fabricmaker (UK) Ltd
Portland House
4 Great Portland Street
London
W1W 8QJ
Tel: 020 7631 3557
Fax: 020 7580 8628
Email: info@johnkaldor.co.uk
www.johnkaldor.co.uk
Beautiful fabrics for dress-making. Check the website for details of stockists

John Lewis
Oxford Street
London
W1A 1EX
Tel: 020 7629 7711
www.johnlewis.com
Stocks a range of dressmaking fabrics, as well as sewing machines, threads and other sewing essentials

Rufflette Ltd (UK)
Sharston Road
Manchester
M22 4TH
www.rufflette.com
Useful website with information on rufflette stockists

Simplicity Ltd (UK)
PO Box 367
Coronation Street
Stockport
Cheshire SK5 7W2
www.simplicity.com
Distributors of Simplicity, New Look and Burda patterns

USA

Brewer Sewing Supplies
19 Evergreen
North Industrial Park
Springfield
TN 37172
Tel: 615 384 1383
Fax: 8880 384 6739
Email:
Stacey@brewersewing.com

Gütermann of America Inc
8227 Arrowridge Blvd
Charlotte
NC 28273
www.gütermann.com

Janome Sewing Machines
10 Industrial Avenue
Mahway
NJ 07430
Tel: 201 825 3200
Fax: 201 825 3612
www.janome.com

Simplicity Pattern Co Inc (USA)
2 Park Avenue, 12th Floor
New York
NY 10016
www.simplicity.com

Textol Systems Inc (Rufflette USA)
435 Meadow Lane
Carlstadt
NJ 07675
www.textol.com

AUSTRALIA

Lincraft
31–33 Alfred Street (Head Off.)
Blackburn
Victoria 3130
Tel: 1800 640 107
www.lincraft.com.au
Major fabric, sewing and craft retailer. Branches nationwide and online supplier

Simplicity Pty Limited
25 Violet Street
Revesby
NSW
Tel: 61 2 9774 5855
Fax: 61 2 9774 3569
Email: info@simp.com.au
www.simp.com.au
Distributors of Simplicity, New Look and Burda patterns

Spotlight
Head Office
100 Market Street
South Melbourne
Victoria 3205
Tel: 1300 305 405
www.spotlight.com.au
Fabric and craft superstores, branches nationwide. Visit the website or phone for mail order delivery

SOUTH AFRICA

Cape Town
Lifestyle Fabrics, Curtain and Linen
11 Picton Road
Parow 7500
Tel/fax: 021 930 5170
Good range of fabric and soft furnishing materials

Durban
Classic Textiles
126 Archary Rd
Clairwood
Durban 4052
Tel: 031 465 9016
Fax: 031 465 9003
Email: info@classictextiles.co.za
www.classictextiles.co.za
A comprehensive range of fabrics, haberdashery and curtaining equipment

NEW ZEALAND

Spotlight Stores
Whangarei (09) 430 7220
Wairau Park (09) 444 0220
Henderson (09) 836 0888
Panmure (09) 527 0915
Manukau City (09) 263 6760
Hamilton (07) 839 1793
Rotorua (07) 343 6901
New Plymouth (06) 757 3575
Gisborne (06) 863 0037
Hastings (06) 878 5223
Palmerston North
    (06) 357 6833
Porirua (04) 238 4055
Wellington (04) 472 5600
Christchurch (03) 377 6121
Dunedin (03) 477 1478
www.spotlight.net.nz
Large selection of fabrics and haberdashery items

Index